LIFE IN THE AGE OF
CHARLEMAGNE

Peter Munz

European Life Series
Edited by Peter Quennell

CAPRICORN BOOKS • New York

Wingate College Library

For Bamboo

First published 1969
© P. Munz 1969
CAPRICORN BOOKS EDITION 1971
Published by arrangement with
B. T. Batsford Ltd, London

Printed in the United States of America

Life in the Age of
Charlemagne

(overleaf) *A Frankish count. Detail from the frescoes in St Benedetto, Malles*

Contents

Preface

This book attempts to describe life and society in the Age of Charlemagne (A.D. 768–814). There are two things which ought to be said by way of preface.

The idea that the Age of Charlemagne has a unity of its own depends entirely upon our knowledge of the towering personality of Charlemagne himself—and that knowledge is almost exclusively based on Einhard's biography of Charlemagne. Einhard wrote his book in the generation after Charlemagne and it is not easy to decide whether his picture was the effect or the cause of the seeming unity of that Age—whether he reflected that unity or whether he created its image. At any rate, it is only proper that the modern historian pays tribute to Einhard by acknowledging that his own work must be based on and be a continuation of Einhard's. In order to remain faithful to the idea of the Age of Charlemagne, I have, with very few exceptions, confined myself strictly to source material which belongs to this period. Since the book was written for a series addressed to the general reader, no references are cited. But every historian acquainted with the period will have no difficulty in identifying the sources I have used.

My debt to modern scholars is immense and so obvious that it is superfluous to mention it. But since this book is not just an exercise in documentary positivism, i.e. a paraphrase of the sources, but aims at a realistic description of how people lived and felt and thought, it is important to state explicitly the general guiding lines I have used in the interpretation of the sources. My interpretation follows a line of thought first indicated by H. Fichtenau in his *The Carolingian Empire*. Fichtenau was led to probe the social and cultural problems of the Age by his recognition that although Charlemagne and his subjects professed to be Christians, they had a very unspiritual grasp of Christianity, coarsened by the primitive nature of social and economic conditions. Fichtenau attributed this coarse unspirituality to the turmoil which had resulted from the dissolution of tribal bonds. I have taken up this suggestion and have explored it more systematically. In this task I have been greatly influenced and helped by what I have learnt from those social anthropologists who have studied similar dissolutions of tribal bonds and corresponding attempts at governmental improvisations, both native and imperial, in nineteenth- and twentieth-century Africa. It seems to me that in the exploration of social relationships the most fruitful results can be achieved by a close co-operation between the social anthropologist and the historian. The historian, without an appreciation of social relationships, is at the mercy of his written sources which are preponderantly literary and legal and which must, therefore, yield a distorted impression of rationality and conscious planning. And without the historian's time dimension, too many of the social anthropologist's descriptions of societies read like descriptions of permanent systems of static order. I am particularly grateful for the encouragement I have received for this line of thought both from F. L. Ganshof, the acknowledged master of Carolingian studies; and from Max Gluckman, Professor of Social Anthropology at the University of Manchester.

Last, but not least, I also owe a great debt to the Deutsche Akademische Austauschdienst through whose generosity I was able to visit the Charlemagne Exhibition in Aix-la-Chapelle in 1965.

P.M.

The Victoria University of Wellington,
New Zealand,
June 1968.

Acknowledgment

The author and publishers would like to thank the following for the illustrations appearing in this book: Aachen Cathedral Treasury for pages 16 and 111; Aachen Stadtbildstelle for pages 3, 20, 24, 50, 51, 109, 139, 145 (top) and 162 (bottom); Alinari for page 159; Alinari-Giraudon for page 84; Biblioteca Apostolica Vaticana for pages 47, 58 and 119; Bibliothèque de l'Arsenal for page 142; Bibliothèque d'Autun for pages 87, 127 and 134; Bibliothèque de Cambrai for pages 39 and 94; Bibliothèque de la Ville, Épernay for pages 17, 53 and 72; Bibliothèque Nationale for pages 22, 90, 95, 129, 137, 138, 155, 164 (left) and 166; Bibliothèque Royale, Bruxelles for pages 108, 113 and 128; Bodleian Library for page 157; Trustees of the British Museum for pages 46, 83, 125, 162 and 163; Burgerbibliothek, Bern for pages 97 and 112; Harald Busch for pages 4, 37 and 52; Cabinet des Médailles for page 60; Civici Instituti di Arte e Storia for page 34; Cividale Museum for page 25; Deutsche Staatsbibliothek, Berlin for page 42; Elek Books Ltd for pages 55, 86 and 104; Foto Marburg for pages 85 and 149; Giraudon for pages 11, 57, 61, 64, 66, 71, 100, 105, 107, 126, 135 and 165; Niko Haas, Trier for page 65; Dr A. Herrnbrodt for page 36; Kunsthistorische Museen, Vienna for page 118; Archives of Modena Cathedral Chapter for page 45; Mansell Collection for pages 71, 77 and 151; Bayer Staatsbibliothek, München for pages 82, 93, 154 and 158; Oesterreichische Nationalbibliothek, Vienna for pages 13, 21, 88, and 124; Oslo University Museum for page 161 (right); Paoletti for pages 160 and 161 (left); Pierpont Morgan Library for page 31; Radio Times Hulton Picture Library for page 63; Romisch-germanisches Zentralmuseum, Mainz for pages 12 and 74; St Procolo, Naturno for page 110; Scala, Milan for page 133; Toni Schneider for page 5; Staatliche Museen, Berlin for pages 27 and 101; Stadtsbibliothek, Trier for pages 75 and 79; Staatsbibliothek, Bamberg for page 116; Hans Steiner for pages 43 and 156; Stiftsbibliothek, Kremsmünster for page 103; Stiftsbibliothek, St Gall for pages 14, 33 and 164 (right); Stuttgart, Würtembergische Landesbibliothek for page 141; Thames and Hudson Ltd for pages 48 and 49; Trinity College, Dublin for page 91; Utrecht University Library for pages 8, 41, 70, 73, 78, 81, 89, 102, 145 (bottom) and 167; Victoria and Albert Museum for pages 15, 18 and 19; Würzburg University Library for page 92.

The author and publishers would also like to thank Constable and Co Ltd for permission to quote on pages 121–3 from Helen Waddell's *Medieval Latin Lyrics*.

The Illustrations

The Illustrations

The Illustrations

The Illustrations

Introduction

On Christmas Day, in the year 800, Charlemagne was acclaimed emperor in Rome. The acclamation was well deserved; for Charlemagne, at that time, was certainly not only the most powerful ruler in Europe but, for all practical purposes, the only ruler. His dominions stretched from the Channel coast to the River Ebro in Spain; from the borders of Denmark to the Côte d'Azur; and from the Atlantic to the River Elbe and, in the south, far into central Italy. They covered almost precisely the whole area of the modern Common Market.

Within this vast area there lived a great variety of people, all at very different levels of development. The centre of gravity of his power was situated in the north, in the triangle between the Rhine, the Moselle and the Meuse. From there it extended to the whole of Gaul, which formed the main body of the kingdom of the Franks to which he had succeeded. By the time Charlemagne was crowned, that kingdom was nominally 300 years old; but except in terms of mere duration, this did not mean much. It had been founded towards the end of the fifth century AD by Clovis, a warrior chieftain of Frankish origin.

The Franks had come into Gaul from across the Rhine. They had come at first under Roman patronage; and later, when Roman power in Gaul was declining, they had come, in very much larger numbers, as invaders. They had migrated in smallish groups and settled all over the country—densely in the north-east and very thinly in the south. Clovis, a particularly enterprising chieftain, had subjected clan after clan to his power. Eventually he had built up a sizeable army and also subjected other Teutonic invaders of Gaul to his power. And finally he emerged as the sole military authority in that ancient Roman province. The Church at first had strongly supported him because he, in turn, was willing to advance the orthodox teaching, i.e. the Nicene Creed, against the various heretical Christian beliefs which had been taken up by the other, non-Frankish invaders of Gaul. Clovis had thus been the champion of the orthodox faith, although in fact he himself was converted to it comparatively late in life. But Clovis was a shrewd man. He

I

saw that his power depended on income; and income was mostly to be had from the taxes to be collected from the flourishing cities of southern Gaul whose wealth depended on Mediterranean trade. These cities were orthodox cities and Clovis wanted to find the approval of their bishops.

Eventually the Church had every reason to regret Clovis's conquest. His warrior bands were more like brigands. They took much and gave nothing in return. But his own power and that of his successors lasted while the citizens of the south paid their taxes. The wealth of those cities began to decline as a result of the decline of Roman power in the Mediterranean. Towards the end of the eighth century, when the conquest of northern Africa and Spain by Islam put an end to all trade in the western Mediterranean, the wealth of these cities disappeared completely and as a result the successors of Clovis ceased to have any importance as rulers of Gaul.

Real power came to be exercised instead by the large, land-owning families of the north. They had their estates and their tenants and retainers and were not dependent on the taxes paid by any subjects. And when, finally, the armies of Islam launched their invasion of Gaul at the beginning of the eighth century and Gaul had to be defended and an army raised, one of those land-owning families was in a position prominent and central enough to undertake the organisation of military defence. This was the Arnulfinger family. (Later they became known as the Carolingians, because of their practice of calling one son in every other generation Charles.) Certain of them had been heads of the household of the old royal family. And at the moment of crisis in the early eighth century, they took the lead not only because they were rich and powerful, but also because they happened, as heads of the royal household, to occupy a position central enough to undertake such a task. At the Battle of Poitiers in 732 Charles the Hammer (Charles Martel) stemmed the Moorish advance into Gaul. And while he was not completely able at that time to secure the southern, Mediterranean coast, he at least prevented a Moorish invasion of Gaul. Pepin, his son and successor, consolidated his strength and in 754, with the full connivance of Pope and Church, unseated the last titular King and heir of Clovis and made himself King of the Franks.

The core of his power lay in the area where he and his family had most of their lands, in the regions of the Meuse, the Moselle and the

Rhine. In that area the other rich families and several bishops and abbots formed a sort of personal association which supported the kingship. From that area royal power stretched by tradition into the other parts of Gaul and was extended, mainly because of lack of concerted and sustained opposition, by Charlemagne, Pepin's son and heir, to the vast bloc described above, so that, by the year 800, it embraced for practical purposes the whole area of the modern Common Market.

But the royal power exercised by Charlemagne was not particularly effective in the more outlying parts of this empire and there were enormous local differences between the various regions. Immediately across the Rhine, there lived the Saxons. They formed a fairly compact tribe. They had never been converted to Christianity and it had taken Charlemagne 30 years to subdue them. He had eventually succeeded because

Bronze statue of Charlemagne

the tribal cohesion of the Saxons was being undermined by fierce internal struggles between the freemen of the tribe and a landed aristocracy, who were the direct descendants of the original Saxons who had invaded the lands between the Rhine and the Weser some centuries before. The aristocracy, anxious to consolidate their ascendancy, sought to undermine popular traditions and institutions, first by inviting and encouraging Christian missionaries and eventually by overtures to the Franks. The upper classes in Saxony, therefore, gravitated towards Charlemagne, while the more common people remained hostile to him and were very reluctant converts to Christianity. With the help of the upper classes the other Saxons had eventually been subdued and the whole region right across to the River Elbe had become subject to Charlemagne.

To the south of Saxony there was the region round the River Main. By contrast to Saxony, royal power had very firm foundations here. The inhabitants had been converted to Christianity almost a century previously. Several bishops and the Abbot of Fulda were large landowners, completely devoted to the King. So were the land-owning families of the region. With the conversion to Christianity and the emergence of the large estates, most local tribal institutions had long been eroded.

Further to the south there lived the Bavarians. Here, in Bavaria, the ancient tribal structure was still fairly strong in spite of the fact that the Bavarians had been Christians for centuries. The Bavarians had lived for a considerable time under the rule of a single tribal chieftain. In 757 their duke, Tassilo, had promised to pay tribute to Pepin, Charlemagne's father. And when Tassilo, for some reason or other, tried to go back on his promise, Charlemagne caused him to be deposed and added Bavaria to his dominions. The incorporation of the Bavarians was easy, for Charlemagne only had to step into the place vacated by Tassilo. But Charlemagne also inherited the fierce expansionist policies of the rich Bavarian families in the east. He had to follow their lead, and attack the heathen Avars who were living to the east of Bavaria.

St Michael, Fulda, Germany

The Avars had been a predatory and nomadic people. They had roamed up and down the Danube basin and held its inhabitants and neighbours to ransom. But, during the decades preceding Charlemagne's conquest, they had already become sedentary and lost most of their brutal fierceness. In following the expansionist trends of the Bavarian families, Charlemagne merely went with the tide, but for obvious reasons official propaganda exaggerated the fierceness of the Avars and the magnitude of their defeat. In fact, the Avars were not organised for determined resistance and collapsed after a minor show of military force. In order to promote the conversion of the people in these lands, Charlemagne appointed a specially trusted friend as Archbishop of Salzburg.

The Tassilo Chalice

Immediately on the other side of the Alps there existed the ancient kingdom of the Lombards. They had for long been a thorn in the side of the Popes—the Lombard Kings and the Lombard princes of central Italy were a constant threat to papal independence in Rome. In 774 it took little persuasion to make Charlemagne invade Lombardy. The Lombards had been settled in northern Italy for some time and, as was the custom, the tribesmen had taken large tracts of land for their own use. But while King succeeded King, the landowners had never formally evolved the habit of giving him suit of court and thus furnishing him with an army. And when Charlemagne's invasion of Lombardy was launched, the King of the Lombards was well-nigh defenceless. Such forces as he had were disbanded and the King sought refuge in Pavia, one of the surviving towns of the region. But from the basis of an urban society and an urban economy, he was powerless to resist Charlemagne's army, which consisted of warriors who were able to provide themselves with armour, horses and men from their landed estates. The 'war' which ensued was a telling commentary. The Lombards held out in both Pavia and Verona. Verona, like Pavia, proved impregnable because its walls, dating from the fourth century, were still in good repair. But Charlemagne was in full command of the countryside and eventually, after nine months, the Lombards in the cities were starved out and the kingdom passed into Charlemagne's hands without fighting.

Turning westwards, we come to central and western Gaul, to the region loosely designated as Aquitaine. Here Charlemagne's power always remained tenuous. The conquest of these regions had been pursued by Charlemagne's father with great determination and ferocity. For the last nine years of his reign, Pepin destroyed city walls and burnt rural estates. In 763 he 'tore up all the vineyards around Issondun'. But Pepin's successes remained precarious. In the very year of his succession, Charlemagne was faced by a revolt in Aquitaine and his ability to crush it was greatly impaired by his brother's open refusal to support him. Aquitaine formed a substantial part of that share of the kingdom which had passed, on Pepin's death, to Carloman, Charlemagne's brother. Carloman did not think it prudent to join Charlemagne against the men on whose support so much of his own power was dependent and to help Charlemagne to increase his power at his, Carloman's, expense. Many years after his brother's death, Charlemagne tried to pour oil on troubled waters by appointing his three-year-old son Louis as sub-king of Aquitaine. Louis was supposed to grow up in Aquitaine and adopt local custom and, though only a sub-king, he was clearly meant to flatter Aquitainian aspirations to independence. Eventually it turned out that Louis was so isolated in Aquitaine that he lacked the necessary supplies of food and clothing. Charlemagne decided to use strong measures, but achieved no more than an arrangement by which four landed estates were set aside for Louis's use. After 778, Charlemagne

excluded the whole of Aquitaine from his itineraries and never again
set foot there.

Finally, in the region of the Pyrenees, Charlemagne had been able to
extend his dominion into northern Spain as far as the River Ebro. In the
780s the inhabitants of Gerona, Urgel and Besalu rebelled against the
authority of the Emir and 'delivered their town to Charles'. Charlemagne could not resist so spontaneous an offer and thus he gradually
occupied the ancient kingdom of the Visigoths, who had settled there in
the early fifth century but had first been defeated by Clovis and later
lost their remaining lands on the south side of the Pyrenees to the
Moorish invaders of Spain. Where the Saxons and Avars had been
heathen and Charlemagne used conversion as a means to exacting
political obedience, the inhabitants of these lands were Christians under
the yoke of the infidel. And in this war of liberation Charlemagne's
warriors were fired by a special religious devotion. These new dominions were a cause of anxiety. The Moors launched general counter-
attacks; Charlemagne had to make special provisions for respecting the
peculiarities of ancient Gothia lest he alienate his new subjects; and in
the end it turned out that the liberated Christians of northern Spain
were still wedded to the off-shoots of the old heresy of Arianism. This
caused a great many doctrinal troubles for Charlemagne and his churchmen.

If all these regions were at different stages of social and religious
development and if there were enormous differences in the efficacy of
Charlemagne's power from region to region, there was one thing all
these areas had in common. Economic life throughout Charlemagne's
dominions was based upon the large landed estate. In some regions this
economy had been an inheritance of the later Roman Empire; in others,
it had grown as a result of the Teutonic migrations and of conquests;
and in yet others, it was a fairly recent development owing to the disintegration of egalitarian tribal life, as in Saxony. The economy of the
large estate gave the whole of Charlemagne's dominions some kind of
economic uniformity. And though each estate was economically fairly
enclosed and self-subsistent and though there was next to no trade and
no economic interdependence, this economy provided some kind of
indirect cohesion for the Empire. For the owners of these estates,
whether lay or clerical, formed an upper layer of society who found it

Besieging a town. Utrecht Psalter

politically prudent and advantageous to be loyal to the King of the Franks, the only viable exponent of military power and the self-styled head of the Christian people. During Charlemagne's long reign (769–814) we know of only two minor conspiracies among some members of this upper land-owning class against his power. The only reason why it took so long to subdue the Saxons was that the upper classes were leaning towards Charlemagne, with the result that the opposition of the lower classes to the upper classes was reflected on Charlemagne himself.

The class of owners of large estates was, however, not yet a real aristocracy in the modern sense of that word. By the nature of the case very few could trace their ancestors back for more than a generation or two, and there were next to no records of the prowess of these ancestors or of their service to king, religion or public. Nor is there any evidence that people at that time were particularly anxious to establish aristocratic dynasties in our sense of the term. None of the writers of the age were commissioned to trace genealogies or write family histories. It is not easy for us today to grasp the extent to which a reputation of 'nobility' depends on the conscious cultivation of records. If we today think of the members of this class as nobility, this is entirely a matter for *our* convenience, and does not reflect the way in which these men thought of themselves. Their only mark of distinction was the fact that their landed property was considerably larger than that of ordinary men.

Nevertheless, it was on the support of members of this class that royal authority rested. And the vast extent of Charlemagne's power depended on the identity of interest of King and large landed property. These men did not owe their landed property to the King's favour. But they knew that, if they obtained a royal office and title, their status in their own region would be much enhanced; and they also knew that, if they accepted an office and title in a distant region, there were new lands and properties that would go with that office. As a result of the enormous spread of Charlemagne's power, the class of landed proprietors became somewhat internationalised. Franks held offices and land in Aquitaine as well as in western Gaul. There were families who held possessions in the region of Paris as well as in central Germany and in Bavaria. One family we happen to know of, the Widones, hailed from the Moselle. Within a single century, members of this family rose to be markgraves of Brittany and dukes of Spoleto.

At the same time it is worth recalling that in the age of Charlemagne the density of population was not very great. It is estimated that on an average there were no more than 10 people to the square kilometre. Only certain parts of the Rhine Valley and the Île-de-France were populated more densely. The great population explosion of the twelfth century was still to come. When the missionary Sturmi travelled through Hesse and Thuringia in the middle of the eighth century he saw nothing but 'wild beasts of which there were a great many; and birds flying and huge trees'. He met human beings only when he walked along well-established tracks, of which there were not many. Most of the land was a frightful wilderness. Organised estates were far apart from one another and separated by thick forests and swamps and from time to time the wanderer would come across a smallish village in which a few peasants lived. But we have no knowledge at all of what life was like in those few independent villages which had not yet become absorbed in a landed estate. Cities, on the other hand, had hardly survived at all. Even in places where people were living on an ancient city site, the economy had sunk to a rural level and the inhabitants were peasants or farmers rather than merchants or manufacturers. There were a few exceptions, but they are hardly notable.

1 The Poor

At the lower end of the social scale there were the poor who tilled the soil. The lands of the abbey of St Germigny-des-Prés near Paris, for example, were divided into a number of subsections, each presided over by a steward. Each subsection was again subdivided. One part was the master's land. On it there was the steward's house, built of stone and containing three or four rooms. It faced an inner court and was surrounded by a number of wooden cottages in which the household servants lived and worked—a kitchen, a bakehouse, barns and stables.

The other part was let out to tenants, whose status was more or less free except that they could not really move away from the land they occupied. This lack of freedom resulted in most cases not from legal obligation but from economic necessity. Each plot was held by one family. The house was smaller than the steward's house and was made of wood. But ploughland and a small vineyard were attached to it. In return for the tenancy, the occupier owed a fixed amount of labour to the steward, and in this way the steward's part of the land was cultivated. The tenant also had to lend a hand in keeping the steward's buildings in repair, carrying loads or cutting down trees. The tenants had to pay dues in kind and delivered firewood, sometimes in return for the privilege of gathering firewood for themselves in the forest, and they had to contribute a sheep for the right to graze their own sheep on the lord's pasture. But there were not only these special rents. The tenant also had to furnish to the steward every year three chickens and 15 eggs, together with a variety of other goods such as wine, honey, wax, soap and oil. On some estates there were tenants who specialised in a craft. There was a blacksmith, a carpenter or a wheelwright and cobblers and on some estates there were men who could make shields for use in war, and carts and litters, and men who could forge weapons. They all had to contribute some of the products of their craft. There were some tenants of such lowly status that they were serfs and in that case even their wives had to give part of the products of their labour, e.g. spun cloth, to the steward.

Exterior of St Germigny-des-Prés

Agricultural production consisted mainly in the various types of grain, such as rye and wheat, barley and oats. It was also necessary to grow plants from which cloth could be made, such as hemp, linen and flax. Horticulture was fairly well developed and a large number of different fruit trees were known. In monastic establishments there was provision for a wide variety of medicinal herbs which were known through classical treatises and again classical tradition caused the cultivation of radishes, onions, horseradishes, pumpkins, lentils, cabbages, leeks, hops and poppyseed. The peasants used shovels and spades, harrows and forks, scythes and sickles, rakes and threshing-sticks. But the most important implement was the plough. It is not clearly known at what time exactly the new type of plough became known in northern Europe. In the ancient Middle East and the Mediterranean lands of the ancient world the soils had been light and people had always used the simple

Reconstruction of a seventh- or eighth-century village

scratch-plough, which consisted of a downward-pointing spike and was drawn by two oxen. It literally merely scratched the soil, first lengthwise and then across, so that the most suitable plot was a square one. The new plough which was coming to be used more and more widely in the northern regions of Europe was a more complicated and efficient instrument. It had a coulter and a ploughshare set so as to cut into the earth. It also had a mould-board which turned the sod sideways and thus formed a ridge and a furrow and in this way served to drain the ground as well as to loosen it. The plough was usually set on a pair of wheels and had to be drawn by a team of oxen. This heavy plough had already been observed by Pliny the Elder in the Alpine regions long before our period. It would seem that in the age of Charlemagne it was very widely used. It was obviously more suitable for the heavy, damp soils of northern Europe than the scratch-plough. Some historians have argued that the introduction of this more efficient plough, which was able to dig deep, turn the sod and provide drainage, must have increased agricultural productivity enormously. But, although it is certain that the heavy plough was widely used in the age of Charlemagne, there is no sign of increased agricultural productivity.

Probably more spectacular at the time than the new plough was the gradual spread of the three-field system of crop rotation. Under the older, two-field system, half the land had been planted with winter grain and the other half had been left fallow. In the following year, the

The Labours of the Months

A cart drawn by oxen from Folchard's Psalter, St Gall

roles of the fields were reversed, so that in every year one-half of the arable land was fallow. In the three-field system, the available land was divided into thirds. One-third was planted in autumn with winter crops (wheat or rye); another was planted in spring with summer crops (oats, barley, lentils); and another was left fallow. In the following year, the first and third fields were planted with summer and winter crops respectively and the second was left fallow, and so on. This new system greatly reduced the land which was left fallow in any one year. This new rotation, with June as the month for ploughing the fallow, was much talked about and attracted great attention—so much so that, when Charlemagne introduced the new vernacular names for the months of the year, June was described as the ploughing month, *Brachmanoth*, and in some ninth-century calendar pictures June is shown as the month in which men plough. Obviously, the ploughing of the fallow land in June was something new and spectacular, which overshadowed the significance of ordinary ploughing for crops at the customary times.

In husbandry, the most common stock was oxen, sheep, pigs and goats. Horses, too, were of great importance and special attention was paid to breeding them for warfare. Oxen and cows were used for food and as draught animals. People also paid some attention to the fact that oxen and cows used as draught animals were not so good for eating— and yet, when animals were scarce, some advised that only lame animals which could not be used for drawing wagons and ploughs should be slaughtered for food. Charlemagne advised his stewards to use the animals of his serfs for ploughing and to preserve his own animals for the table. The fat of animals was used in the preparation of food. Butter was known, but considered a rarity. People made bacon, smoked meat and sausages. Cheese, fish and vegetables were used mainly for the fast-days and during Lent. But obviously meat cannot have been the staple food of the poorer people. Charlemagne, on the other hand, was a great

The Annunciation. The Angels appear to the shepherds guarding their flocks. From the ivory bookcover of the Lorsch Gospels

meat-eater and it was a rule that each of his many domains had to furnish every year at least two fat oxen to the royal palace.

There was also a great deal of viticulture. In some of Charlemagne's instructions there were special provisions for the making of wine. It was forbidden to press the grapes with feet and the wine was to be stored in sound barrels with iron hoops. He did not like wine to be sent to the palace in leather bottles. Apart from wine, people made beer, mulberry wine, cider and mead. Water was drunk only by the poor. For the wealthier people the main drink was beer, *cervisia*, made from sprouting barley.

On the royal estates, the women's quarters were surrounded by hedges. In their lodgings, the women busied themselves weaving and sewing clothes. There was supposed to be a fireplace to keep them warm in their sedentary occupation. They wove linen, combed wool, and dyed cloth. The estate was, therefore, self-sufficient even so far as clothing was concerned.

These great estates were 'vast concerns, farms and factories, all in one'. The economic efficiency of these enterprises depended very much on two factors. First, there had to be a certain amount of skill in the various crafts. The monks of St Germigny-des-Prés kept a number of skilled craftsmen in the vicinity of the main monastery so that they would be able to obtain their products directly. If the monks were lucky, they would obtain the services not only of the ordinary craftsmen but also of a silversmith, a mason and an ebony-carver. But these latter skills were very rare and their owners would be able to hire themselves out to the highest bidder. Sometimes a bishop would, as a special favour, send the practitioner of such a skill to another bishop or abbot. In an instruction for the administration of his own estates, Charlemagne prescribed that the steward was to take care to have skilled craftsmen in each district. The list is re-

Detail from an ivory diptych

vealing: there was to be a blacksmith, a goldsmith, a silversmith,
a shoemaker, a turner, a carpenter,
a swordmaker, a soapmaker, fisher-
men, foilers and netmakers, as well
as men who knew how to make
beer. The level of production was
extremely low and the only skills
required were those necessary to
the running of the estate. Nobody
thought in terms of producing
goods for a distant market or even
for barter with a neighbouring
estate. Each estate was self-sufficient
and represented a closed economy.

Man working on the roof of a building

Masons, silversmiths, goldsmiths and
ebony-carvers were rare and produced luxury goods—not for sale but
for the benefit of the bishop or abbot whose estates were large enough to
support men with such skills.

Such trade as there was was on the whole highly specialised. Traders
from the city of Mainz sometimes travelled up the Main to buy corn.
On the Danube there were ships carrying salt and traders carrying furs
from the forests in the east to the west. On a more local scale, there
was the yearly fair of St Denys near Paris, where merchants offered rare
goods from distant lands in exchange for corn, wine and honey produced
locally. But the traders in salt and fur and the fair of St Denys were
exceptional. Their existence does not entitle us to describe the economy
of the age of Charlemagne as anything but rural and self-sufficient.

The second factor on which the efficiency of the estate depended was
a personal one. The tenant would naturally tend to work harder when
ploughing his own land than when ploughing for the steward. But the
steward could inflict penalties and make himself unpleasant in many
other ways. He could even have the tenant flogged. Personally, tenants
and steward were very dependent on each other. The peasant might
try to bribe the steward to be let off a burdensome task, but the steward
who was known to be just and equitable was more likely to get the best
results from the tenant.

The Nativity from the ivory

   As so often in human affairs, common sense did not prevail widely.
Stewards were harsh and exploited rather than cajoled the tenant. Many
freemen and serfs ran away from their masters—in an astrological
calendar the days especially favourable for escaping were marked. Even
the King's stewards were corrupt. An abbot who had been appointed
supervisor of the royal building works at Aix-la-Chapelle enriched himself by releasing all those men who were able to offer a bribe and, to
make up for the loss of labour, he exploited the strength of the remaining
men to the utmost. In this particular case the men seem to have resorted
to self-help. The house in which the abbot had stored his ill-gotten
riches was razed to the ground and the abbot, while attempting to save
his hoard, was burnt to death. Charlemagne himself refused to interfere.
Like Charlemagne, the majority of landowners allowed things to work
themselves out. Most owners, though they preferred their stewards not
to accept bribes, found it in their own interest to allow some kind of

bookcover of the Lorsch Gospels

balance to work itself out in relations between steward and tenant so that production did not decline. There was, therefore, a very wide variety in the efficiency of these estates and that efficiency depended ultimately on these personal factors.

Since every estate was more or less a closed economy, it was extremely vulnerable to droughts and floods or any other natural disaster which might befall the district. In some cases stewards tried to provide against such disasters by arranging for the storage of the less perishable goods and there were even cases where the inhabitants of one estate helped those of a neighbouring estate. But there was no point in organising production with a view to the exchange of goods, because if one estate was in trouble the neighbouring estates were likely to be in trouble too for the same reason. And the more distant estates were, for practical purposes, out of reach because of the absence of good roads and means of transport. Hunger and disease were rampant. In 791 there was a

eprofuf

Christ healing the leper

famine which led to cannibalism and some people even ate members of their own family. In 800 it was reported that one plague followed another, and in 797 Alcuin, the Abbot of St Martin's, recorded that his own body-servant had run away because of hunger and added that there was so little food around the house that he had needed it all himself.

The life of the lower classes was certainly far from idyllic. Just as it is impossible to see the land-owning upper classes as a legally distinct estate of nobility, so it is also impossible to classify the members of the lower classes along strictly legal lines. A very large number of them were supposed to be free or were descended from freemen. In St Germigny-des-Prés, for instance, for every clearly servile household, there were 23 belonging to freemen or manumitted serfs. But this meant very little. If a man was a tenant, be it of a monastery, a bishop or a secular magnate, it did not matter much for practical purposes what his exact legal status in regard to freedom was. His status and his freedom depended on his economic condition. The poorer he was and the smaller his holding, the more likely he was to be treated as a serf or a villein.

In the absence of clearly defined legal status and given the fact that there were no clear registers and records, there was, of course, a great deal of mobility among the lower classes. But for the most part mobility meant a constant tendency for the poorer people to descend in the social scale. It was in the interests of stewards and masters of all kinds to increase the exactions that were due and thus depress the status of the tenant, who had no means of protesting other than running away. But, when he had a family, his chance of running away cannot have been very great. However, descent in the social scale was not only due to the increased pressure of lords and masters. Often enough it was voluntary. As Charlemagne's wars increased and military service came to be demanded more and more frequently, many poor people sought to avoid it (theoretically, only freemen were liable) by seeking servitude of some kind or another. They would voluntarily surrender their plot to a powerful landowner and receive it back from him as a tenancy. They received less than they had surrendered and, in addition, were likely to owe services as well. But at least they could now reasonably hope to avoid military service in distant lands.

The voluntary formation of such bonds of dependence was also advantageous in other respects. When a poor man was summoned before a court of law, there was no hope that his testimony would prevail against that of the powerful and rich men of the district who were, more-over, likely to be related to the presiding count. But a poor man who was a rich man's vassal could count on his lord's protection in court. At the same time these arrangements were open to gross abuse because they led to regular 'protection rackets': a poor man could be forced into a rich man's vassalage by the threat that he might be hauled in to a court of law on a trumped-up charge. His prospective lord might be the count's cousin or brother.

On many occasions the poor and defence-less resorted to self

Phases of the moon and sun, and the signs of the zodiac

SOROR mea FLOREN
TINA accipe codicem
Quemtibi compo
Sui feliciter
Amen

Isidor and his sister

help. In ancient tribal society, the Franks had known the habit of forming ritual oath-guilds. The habit had persisted but tended to acquire a more purely utilitarian character. People would now form such a guild to help each other in case of fire or famine and would choose a saint as a patron. Such associations could also be directed against the powerful men in the district and as such they were suspect, for they were an alternative to the formation of those feudal bonds of dependence of which the magnates were the material benificiaries, whatever the protection which might accrue from them to the poor. Such oath-guilds for mutual help against the rich were frequent in regions where the acquisitive appetites of the rich were particularly strong and where an unusual number of freemen had been forced into servitude or vassalage. In some cases such guilds even became downright conspiracies. But there is no sign that they ever led to anything which might be described as a social revolt.

In some cases there was also a possibility of an ascent of the social ladder. There were estates which were not very centrally administered. On such estates, the tenants of the outlying plots would often be left very much to themselves and, if they were enterprising, they might be able to make their neighbours dependent on themselves and enlarge their holdings by clearing a bit of forest or draining a swamp.

Another possibility of rising in the social scale was to be appointed as a lord's steward. In most cases the office of stewardship was hereditary and a son could expect to succeed his father, but new stewards were often needed and they could be recruited only from the ranks of the lower classes. A lord would often be tempted to choose as his steward a man who came from a very lowly family—the fact that he owed his social status to the lord meant that there was a better chance of his remaining loyal. However, a steward had to have some kind of elementary and practical education; he had to have some knowledge of agriculture, husbandry and viticulture; and at times he was required to have enough knowledge of writing to be able to write accounts. Such knowledge was very hard to come by. There were no schools and no priests who could impart it. And this fact tended to make the stewards into a special class. The wealthier ones, and especially those in charge of the more prosperous estates, were men who tried to have their sons taught these elementary skills in the Palace Schools organised by the King. Charlemagne himself commented on the fact that these boys were more eager pupils than the sons of the members of the upper classes.

As a result of economic depression, natural disasters and social exploitation, there was a vast wayfaring population throughout Charlemagne's dominions. When he built his capital in Aix-la-Chapelle, Charlemagne had to appoint special bailiffs in charge of the beggars. Some lived on their wits and performed tricks for the entertainment of the wealthier people. Others lived on alms. Some exhibited their real or pretended deformities as a source of amusement. There were jugglers and minstrels, often welcome for the night in a manor-house or in the royal palaces. Some traded in relics which were very much in demand and others were vagrants and thieves. Life on the highways was always precarious. There were slave-traders who caught people and sold them into Spain, where slavery under Islam was an established institution. People were murdered; and, being unattached, the murderer never had to fear retribution from the members of his victim's family. Many of

Hercules killing a snake

the unattached, wayfaring people would pretend to be clerks or pilgrims in order to enjoy such protection as the cloak of religion might offer.

The lower classes were not only desperately poor and helpless. They were also totally uneducated, and completely illiterate. Worse still, they were prey to the most appalling superstitions. Nominally they were all Christians. Even in Saxony, where conversion was not really begun until after the turn of the century, it progressed very rapidly within a single decade. But such conversion to Christianity did not mean much—on the contrary, its victims suffered the worst of both worlds. They lost, together with their ancient tribal structure and ritual, the moral sanctions which had been built into their old religion. And since the new religion was only superficial and not backed by any kind of theological education, they failed to benefit from the spiritual exhortations which we associate with Christianity. The result was that these people nourished the last remnants of rank paganism with the thinnest Christian veneer. People performed sacrifices in honour of the spirits of trees, stones and springs. They worshipped animate as well as inanimate nature. They believed that the whole world was full of spirits which ought to be placated. People paid fees to weather-wizards who promised to protect them against thunderstorms.

Superstitions about magic and soothsayers were rampant. In his effort to assist the progress of Christianity, Charlemagne legislated severely against the belief in witchcraft and sorcery, and people who held such beliefs were to be punished as severely as those who claimed to be able to practise sorcery and witchcraft. In the books of penance, people who consulted magicians and soothsayers were subjected to the same penance as people who were guilty of manslaughter. But all in vain: the magical arts flourished and ministered to the spiritual and psychological needs of people who had lost their ancient tribal rituals and mythology and had gained nothing solid in return because the Church was not sufficiently well organised to fill the gap. In the Lyon region the belief that evil men had arrived on 'airships' (a kind of medieval 'flying-saucer'?) was widespread. These men were supposed to have been sent by the sorcerers of Magonia to steal the harvest. On one occasion three men and a woman gathering fruits in a field devastated by a gale were arrested and sentenced to be stoned. The Bishop wrote with anger of 'this false belief which has gained such an ascendancy over practically everyone in the region'. Strangers were often seized and stoned because they were held responsible for a plague, a drought or a cattle disease, or suspected of poisoning wells or pastures.

In many parts, people simply continued the observation of pagan cults. Sacrifices for the dead, sorcery and animal sacrifices were widely practised. The purification fire ritual performed on the occasion of the solstice was particularly popular. So was the ancient pagan custom of the ritual dance. It was frequently

Christ in Majesty, Cividale Cathedral, Italy

practised in front of churches and on the occasion of an assembly gathered to administer justice. One can easily see the strength of the survival of pagan tribal custom. Both a religious and a judicial gathering could not be validated without the performance of a communal dance. The authorities who objected and who wanted to exclude such communal traditions from Christian meetings and from the 'rational' administration of justice met with bitter opposition. The lives of the lower classes, prey to such hatreds and such imaginings, were fairly nasty and brutish and, for the most part, short.

To seek protection from demons and strangers people turned to the worship of saints. Not only did they worship eagerly the saints prescribed by the Church, but they were also prone to worship recently deceased local inhabitants. The practices and cults administered by the clergy did not afford much consolation. If there was a church on the estate in which a priest performed the prescribed ceremonies, he was likely to be so ignorant himself as to perform them in a very improper and abbreviated manner. Popular superstition itself militated against the sacraments. People believed that the flesh and blood of the heavenly Lord were so holy and so imbued with magic power that they could not be swallowed. The whole symbolism of Christianity was shorn of its transcendental meaning and the mystery of creation, death and resurrection was forgotten. In the popular imagination Christ was presented as a King—a heavenly ruler. He was never presented as the Son of Man, suffering on the cross. The mystery of the Resurrection disappeared behind a cloud of magic.

Popular religion, in so far as it was directly concerned with Christianity at all, consisted in the worship of relics. The bones of a saint or martyr were something tangible. When the relics of a saint were transferred, people remarked about the sweet smell of the corpse. At first a coffin might be too heavy to be moved at all; eventually it moved into its new tomb of its own accord. Relics consisted of single bones or splinters of bones; sometimes of a whole corpse. Such relics could work miracles and cure diseases. The new religion, owing to the absence of teachers and the complete illiteracy of the people, was not able to afford any kind of spiritual guidance or transcendental comfort. People were eagerly content with the crudest kind of magic, and the miracles worked by a saint, a relic of a saint, or a tomb of a saint.

People crowded round these tombs and carried splinters of relics, if they could afford them, in little bags round their necks. This was the only kind of protection they believed in and the only kind of mental comfort and sustenance which had any meaning for them. And once these religious customs and manners were established, they were never again completely abandoned. We must always try to remember that

Reliquary of Engern

many parts of medieval Christianity were evolved and fashioned under those conditions. They were not developed by theologians and spiritually perceptive people, but by people who had lost their old tribal religion and its institutions; and lived at a time when the Church was so disorganised that it could not provide even the most elementary guidance and instruction.

Relics were not too hard to come by. Since there was no official method by which genuine saintliness was defined, a man's reputation for saintliness depended entirely on the popular response. There were a few tombs of genuine martyrs from ancient Roman times. But in the three centuries preceding the age of Charlemagne, hundreds of places began to be worshipped as the tombs of people who had acquired a reputation for saintliness. Some had been hermits, some renowned virgins, some had been missionaries who had been martyred and others had been simple clerics without claim to special distinction. And others again were worshipped because they contained the bones of a member of a wealthy family who promoted the cult because it helped to consolidate their social position. A church could only draw a crowd if it contained relics, and there was hardly a diocese in existence which did not contain relics as its religious focus. When Angilbert, one of Charlemagne's courtiers and magnates, built his monastic church at Centula not far from the modern Crécy in Normandy, he designed the church so that it could accommodate nearly 100 relics. It became, in fact, one of the most renowned centres of Carolingian religious magic. Each relic had its altar and each altar was serviced by an elaborate liturgy performed by 300 monks and 100 clerics.

With the growing demand for relics, the local supply tended to dry up. There was fierce competition and nobody was willing to share his relics or to divide a corpse. As a result the attention of professional traders turned to Rome, the city which was known to be 'red with the blood of martyrs' and where the supply of relics was almost unlimited. But the Roman authorities soon took precautions. Relics attracted people; and there was a constant stream of people journeying to Rome to worship at the tombs of the martyrs. This stream of pilgrims enhanced the standing of the Bishop of Rome. In 761 Pope Paul I ordered a great many of these bones to be transferred from their original resting-places in the suburbs into the centre of the city where they would be safe; while in 817 Pope Paschal I had another 2,300 corpses of saints and martyrs transferred from the outlying districts into the city. But traders always managed to dig up more and, although it was prohibited to export relics from Rome without papal permission, there was ample scope for smuggling and for fraud. We have a very elaborate description by Einhard, one of Charlemagne's friends and scholars, of the incredible difficulties, the unctuous dishonesty and the hazards of this trade. Through Einhard we know of a Roman deacon, one Deusdona, who seems to have been a professional relic trader, a man fairly typical of his class. He lured two of Einhard's servants, Ratleik and Hun, to Rome with the prospect of letting them have several precious relics, only to involve them in endless fraudulent tergiversations. Eventually Einhard's servants managed to lay their hands on some relics and, after further delays and many perils, they succeeded in delivering their precious treasures to their master. There were night visits to the Catacombs and attempts to rifle tombs—all carried out under the cloak of secrecy because the violation of tombs was punishable by death. The whole account reads like a first-class Gothic novel.

The enthusiastic worship of relics and their power to work miracles was no doubt able to fill the large gap left in people's lives by the disappearance of their ancient pagan religion. But apart from this worship there was very little to show on the positive side as far as the lower classes were concerned. The peasants were interested in the fertility of the soil and of their animals, in the seasons and the weather. The formal adoption of Christianity tended to weaken their traditional ritual and whatever they took up from the new religion had to be bent to serve their urgent emotional preoccupations which were of necessity very different from those of the urban population of the ancient Mediterranean world among whom Christianity had first been developed. The authorities, though extremely uneasy about the strength of the surviving pagan cults, were not sufficiently far removed from the peasant mentality and the rural economy to devise very effective antidotes.

2 The Rich

At the other end of the social scale there were the upper classes. But in one important respect their lives did not differ from those of the lower classes. They, too, were completely illiterate and uneducated and were prey to the same superstitions which were mushrooming in the no-man's-land between ancient paganism and the new religion. They had greater means to acquire relics and they often made donations to the Church in order to acquire merit in the eyes of God; and often enough they set land aside in order to erect a church and support a priest. In their own eyes, therefore, they must have appeared as having a some-what greater chance of finding the favour of the heavenly powers than the lower classes, who could neither afford many relics nor make many donations to the Church and who often found difficulty even in paying tithes to the priests. But if their protection against the powers of dark-ness was thus slightly greater, their educational level and their under-standing of the world was hardly different from that of the poor peasants who supported them. It is a remarkable fact, and one that is all too often forgotten, that the moral influence of Christianity and the softening of personal manners and habits did not begin until a social framework was evolved for it. Only when feudalism had struck firm roots and defined the principles of mutual obligation between lord and vassal and instilled into both lord and vassal the ideals of courtly and chivalrous behaviour; only when the growth of city life provided an environment which was based on co-operation and mutual respect among the citizens—only then did Christian ideals of brotherly love acquire some reality. But in the age of Charlemagne the influence of Christianity was hardly notice-able among the lower and the upper classes of the population, apart from a few very rare exceptions.

The worst result of the failure of the Christian religion to instil gentler and more peaceful habits and ideals of equity, not to speak of charity and the forgiving of trespasses, however, was to be found not among the poor peasants, but among the upper classes—the upper classes had so many more opportunities to be brutal and aggressive. For

Silver jewelled front cover of the Lindau Gospels

the most part, the King and his officers of justice, such as they were, were too far away to be a restraining influence, and consequently the upper classes were left fairly free to indulge their appetites for acquisition and exploitation. And since members of the upper classes lived with their families on large estates far removed from each other, they no longer shared a communal life and were no longer subject to the moral pressures and restraints of the communal organisation of a clan or a tribe.

There was no clear definition of the membership of this upper class. It was generally held that there was an upper stratum of men who were referred to as *potens*—men of power, or magnates. Power was measured entirely in terms of landed wealth. An office-holder might also qualify as a *potens*, but only if he used the opportunities offered by his position to acquire land, i.e. not by virtue of the office itself. All this generated an atmosphere of brutal acquisitiveness among the members of the upper classes. They were all people out to grasp land for themselves and the members of their family and to enlarge what they had grasped. Looked at psychologically this is understandable enough—for the acquisition of land was the only channel in which the acquisitive instinct could mani-fest itself; and, furthermore, in an age in which there was no room for education or the more sophisticated diversions of culture, the acquisition of land also became the only pastime.

The principle of private and individual property was nothing new in the age of Charlemagne. For several centuries the older tribal concept of the communal ownership of land had been abandoned. There had emerged, instead, the principle of private property, known as the *alod* in Germany and in Gaul and as *bookland* in England. It was very similar to what the Romans had called *possessio*—landed property over which an individual had full and exclusive rights.

This change in the nature of the ownership of land had been brought about by the dissolution of the ancient tribes during the centuries of migration. As the Franks moved into Gaul, they would conquer and occupy new lands. Their clans were dissolving and thus any chieftain would reward his mightiest and bravest warriors with a piece of land. In the new country, the land could hardly be owned communally by a tribe, a clan or a hundred. The successful chieftains always took the lion's share; but their own power depended on the support of their warriors and it was therefore in their own interest to share the booty. They not only had to share the booty; once shared, they also found it impossible ever to touch it again. Their power depended on their followers' co-operation rather than on an institution. And this co-operation could only be ensured if every magnate's property rights were inviolable. Even when in a case of gross disloyalty an individual magnate had to be eliminated, his lands were left intact for his heirs or kinsmen.

The acquisition of such properties resulted from conquest, usurpation

Taking a town. Golden Psalter, St Gall

and encroachments on more ancient communal rights to the land. The disintegration of tribal solidarity and communal ownership was countenanced and accelerated by two factors. First and ironically, the acceptance of Christianity militated against such traditional ethical concepts as honour and loyalty and therefore cleared the way for a more brutal individualism without being able to instil the new values of forgiveness and charity. Christianity first of all acted as a powerful solvent

A folding stool

of traditional tribal morality. It created, or helped to create, the conditions which would have made a resort to charity and forgiveness more necessary than it had been when lives were more regulated by tribal custom and tribal sanctions. But at that very moment it failed to propagate the new values and left the Franks in a moral no-man's-land.

In many parts of Gaul the Franks found on their arrival the institution of the large landed estate already in full swing. The ancient Roman senatorial families formed something like a landed aristocracy in Gaul and the Frankish newcomers simply took over some of their estates and learnt very easily to imitate their acquisitive habits and accepted the remnants of this senatorial class as their equals. The early Frankish Kings considered the administrative officials of the Roman senatorial aristocracy as the equals of their own officials whom they used to run their own estates. And the custom of having a fortified palace or manor-house in the centre of the estate goes back in many parts of Gaul to the late third century, that is to the age of Roman power.

In this way, we can watch how opportunity countenanced the growth of brutality; and how the brutality generated by the disappearance of tribal sanctions and clan solidarity countenanced further acquisitions. The landed properties thus built up often reached enormous proportions. It has been estimated that, while in Gaul in ancient Roman days an estate might consist of 900 hectares, an estate in the early days of Frankish conquest might include as many as 1,800 or even 2,600 hectares. The Duke of Bavaria possessed as many as 276 manses (households) in one district and 100 in another. And there were many cases where the landed property of one man was scattered over many regions. We know, for example, of one, Isanbert, whose family had hailed from as far east as modern Austria. He himself was born in Gascony, grew up in eastern Francia and eventually became a monk in the monastery of

Fulda in eastern Franconia. As the estates grew and one man came to own properties in a large number of different regions, he was bound to become uprooted. He would lose connections with soil and people; and this lack of attachment would further encourage a lack of restraint and rid him of the sense of shame or guilt to which continued links with clan or tribe would have subjected him. The ideal opportunity for a free indulgence of the acquisitive instinct came when a magnate was made a count. The main duty of a count was to raise an army for the King in the county. This duty made it possible for the count to blackmail and exploit the inhabitants of the county by constantly threatening to call them up and offering to let them off in return for favours. The victim might have to transfer his property to the count, become his vassal or serf (according to the size of the property) or be invested with that property or part of it in the form of a tenure subject to rents in services and kind.

But the results of this acquisitiveness were not wholly negative. In an age in which the King was far away and when the absence of a civil service and the enormous difficulties of communication made it impossible for him to assert his restraining influence or encourage some small measure of equitable justice in more than one small region at a time, all but the most brutal and aggressive people found it advantageous to seek the protection of a powerful, that is, wealthy, man. In this way the acquisitive drives of the upper classes found sudden and spontaneous support in the natural desire for security and protection of the lower orders. They would rush to commend their lands and their persons to a magnate and thus minister voluntarily to his desire to increase his holdings. When a poor man thus commended himself to a powerful man, he would receive back part of his lands as a *precarium* or a *beneficium*—as a tenure burdened by specified conditions of service and loyalty. At first such arrangements were temporary, but by the nature of the case they generally tended to become hereditary. And in this way the bonds of society came to be formed not by the simple relationship between King and his subjects, but by the relationship between a lord and his vassals. The King, far from objecting, countenanced these developments, for they tended to weld the many people who lived in his dominions into a social fabric. Otherwise there would have been no social integration at all. The King's dominions would have been filled

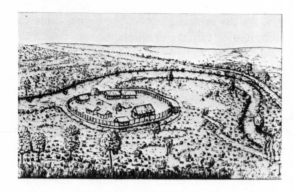

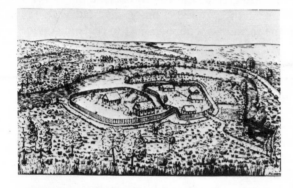

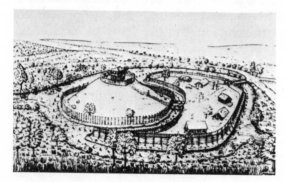

Three stages in the development of a ninth-century villa

entirely by individual atoms preying on each other and by internecine struggles.

This kind of incipient feudalism developed some new vertical bonds of association. But there were also signs of the growth of horizontal bonds which tied some members of the upper classes into groups and associations and made them feel that they belonged together and had obligations to each other over and above those owed to their family and their King (to whom they were tied mainly by a cool calculation of their own interests). If the new religion signally failed to provide moral sanctions and ideals, it did provide two special institutions, the drinking association and the prayer association. Ritual communal drinking had been an old pagan custom. It was adopted by the

Christianity of the age in a slightly different form. Men would gather on holy days to sing a hymn to a saint and the hymn would end with an invitation to drink his health. One is not far wrong in thinking that rituals of this kind were more widespread and more punctiliously observed than the celebration of the Mass. They offered an occasion for people to celebrate and to congregate.

The gateway of Lorsch monastery

The prayer association was less immediate in its social effect; but it nevertheless constituted a powerful bond between people of the same class. Again, following an old tribal custom of swearing together to form an association, people founded 'confraternities for the dead'. On one occasion the bishops and abbots of Bavaria formed such an association 'for the benefit of dead brothers'. On the death of any member, each surviving member was to have 100 Masses sung for him. Such prayer confraternities eventually formed a network which not only covered the whole Empire, but sometimes stretched beyond its boundaries into Spain and England. Their existence is not a proof of an intensely personal spiritual life; but they served a useful purpose in linking people together horizontally.

If the King's policy, the magnate's acquisitive appetites and the poor man's need for protection tended to coincide, the result could be beneficial to all concerned. But we do know of a great many cases of excessive hardship and oppression and the poor often groaned under ever-increasing exploitation. One of Charlemagne's sons-in-law, Bego, enjoyed a particularly sinister reputation. He was one of the most powerful men in Aquitaine. After his death an old woman who had no doubt suffered from his brutality had a vision. She saw hellish demons pouring liquid gold into Bego's mouth and heard them saying: 'All your life you have been thirsting for such gold without ever being able to quench your thirst: you can quench it now!'

The large domain was usually known as a *villa*, but also as a *manor*, *curtis*, *sala* or *fundus*. It was a self-sufficient economic organisation. At its centre there was the lord's dwelling, known as the *palatium* or the *castellum*. This was a cross between a large farmhouse and a castle and was surrounded by a wooden stockade. It contained a banqueting hall, sleeping quarters, cellars, stables and storehouses and a small chapel. If a magnate owned more than one villa, he would also have more than one such palace and would spend part of his time in one and part of his time in the other. He lived on the proceeds of the villa, and, since they could neither be transported nor turned into cash, he was compelled by economic necessity to be personally present, together with the members of his family, for at least part of the year.

The administration of these domains differed. We know that those of the King were subject to the most minute and careful regulation and that the stewards were issued with detailed instructions about tenants' liabilities, the organisation of work, and the standards of cleanliness to be observed in the making of salted meat, cheeses, butter and honey. It was also laid down that on each estate the chambers were to be provided with counterpanes, cushions, pillows and bedclothes. There had to be vessels of brass, iron and lead, chains and pot-hooks and a specified number of tools such as adzes, axes and cutlasses. The steward also had to provide a number of weapons, to care for them and to make sure that after use they were to be kept in good condition and stored in the chamber.

On one royal estate there was a house, built of stone 'in the best manner', with three rooms and surrounding balcony. There were 11 apartments for women, one cellar, two porticoes, 17 other houses built of wood within the courtyard, one stable, one kitchen, one mill, one granary and three barns. The yard itself was surrounded by a hedge and entered by a stone gateway, above which was a balcony from which distributions could be made. (One such gateway has been preserved to the present day in the village of Lorsch near the Rhine, opposite the city of Worms. This one did not have a balcony but contained, on the upper floor, a real reception hall.) There was also to be an inner yard, again enclosed by a hedge and planted with various kinds of trees.

We know nothing about how the members of the upper classes spent their leisure. Life must have been incredibly boring during the long winter evenings. A wayfaring minstrel or a juggler would be welcome; but for the most part the only likely entertainment was drinking and there was certainly a great deal of drunkenness.

Some of the garments worn by the upper classes were derived from Roman styles. The main garment consisted of a tunic which came down to just above the knees. For greater protection against the cold they would wear a kind of toga fastened on one shoulder by a brooch.

A saint with armed men

Boots made of leather were known, but they were very hard to come by (one of Charlemagne's officials found it worth recording that on one occasion he was offered a pair as a bribe). But the style of clothing also showed ancient Frankish features. Charlemagne himself dressed in a linen shirt and linen underpants, over which he wore a silk-embroidered vest covered with fur in winter for greater warmth. He also wore shortish trousers. His legs were covered by bandaged leggings and on his feet he wore shoes which resembled sandals. All these articles of clothing were utilitarian and home-made and there was no scope for luxurious display of finery or for fashion consciousness.

3 The King

Foremost among the upper-class families was the royal family, presided over by the King himself in typically patriarchal fashion. One can easily understand why Charlemagne should have found more in common with the ancient Jewish patriarchs and Kings of the Old Testament than with other Biblical heroes. Like the ancient Biblical patriarchs he, too, led a nomadic life. True, he did not live entirely in tents and he did not take his herds with him. But he, too, together with his family, spent most of his life perambulating from one of his palaces to another—he had no income to speak of other than the food and the products provided by these estates. The estates of his family were situated all over his dominions, but the closest concentration was in the triangle between the Rhine, the Meuse and the Moselle.

The royal palaces on these estates were more splendid than those of the average upper-class family. It is remarkable, and perhaps a sign of the greater peacefulness of the age of Charlemagne, that most of them were not heavily fortified. Charlemagne also used to spend time in the palaces of his bishops or abbots and in some of these places a special royal palace was erected to accommodate him. Sometimes he had to take up his residence in places where he was conducting a campaign and then his itinerary might take him far afield, into Lombardy, Bavaria or Saxony. But when he was not on the warpath, he preferred to spend his time in his favourite palaces. There were approximately 35 winters in his life (he ruled for 45 years) during which he could take up a leisurely residence somewhere. He spent three of them in Worms, two in Diedenhofen, two in Attigny, three in Qierzy, five in Heristal and probably 18 in Aix-la-Chapelle which, from the end of the eighth century quickly became his favourite place of residence. Wherever he took up his residence he found himself in the circle of his large family.

The whole tenor of his life showed that he loved life and worldly pleasure. On important days there were banquets. Charlemagne was exceedingly fond of good food. He preferred roast savoury venison, hot from the spit, and disliked boiled meat. Whenever possible, he went

Life at Court from the Utrecht Psalter

hunting. He loved hunting. On the appointed day, Charlemagne appeared on his favourite horse, splendidly saddled. There was the sound of the horns and the barking of dogs and the attendants followed with spears and nets. His wife and daughters often joined him, delighting in their beauty and physical vigour. Charlemagne was always in the front and the prey was divided equally. The party rested in a clearing in the forest. There were tents and food and drink. The hunt often ended with a banquet in a hunting-lodge: there was much eating and drinking and sexual pleasures were freely indulged in. In this respect there was a remarkable contrast between his own reign and that of his son and successor, when a cloud of dour puritanism descended upon the Frankish Court (no doubt something of a reaction against what had gone before). According to gossip there was only one woman in Charlemagne's circle who did not succumb to these temptations. There was a constant coming and going of jugglers, jesters and minstrels whom Charlemagne encouraged because they would spread his fame in other countries and at other Courts. Charlemagne was not much given to solitary meditation and reflection upon affairs of state. He seems to have been fully himself in this convivial atmosphere and according to one observer a minstrel's song recited at an opportune moment could make him change his mind on important affairs of state.

But one should not conclude that life at Charlemagne's Court was frivolous. Charlemagne hated drunkenness and, unless there was a banquet, he not only liked to be entertained by minstrels when he was eating but often ordered that someone should read to him from historical works or from the writings of St Augustine, especially the *City of God*. He was very fond of intellectual stimulus. He discussed questions of theology and ecclesiastical administration. He argued with the Court scholars about rhetoric and astronomy and, wherever he happened to be, he talked about military campaigns or administration. At table someone would read a poem which was then discussed and often a poem of thanks was composed there and then, with everybody present contributing a verse.

His conviviality, however, was carried to great lengths. Not only was he pleased to see people who happened to drop in, but he also encouraged people to be present when he was dressing or having his bath, and he clearly enjoyed company, noise, activity and commotion. In Aix-la-Chapelle he gave parties in the swimming-pool fed by the mineral springs. He seemed happiest among the din of the hunt or supervising in person the building activities which he was promoting in Aix-la-Chapelle.

There was also opportunity for light-hearted entertainment. Charlemagne once played a trick on a foolish bishop who was a great collector

St Augustine

Statue of Charlemagne at the east end of St John's, Müstair, Switzerland

of silly curios. A merchant was ordered to wrap a dead mouse in a precious silk cloth and the poor bishop bought it for a full pound of silver as a rare animal. The merchant then handed over the money to Charlemagne, who held up the bishop to public ridicule. On another occasion, when some of his companions appeared for the hunt in unsuitably ornate garments, Charlemagne in person led them through thick growth so that they returned with their clothes torn. Charlemagne himself preferred very simple garments and only on very special occasions used special decorations for purposes of political display. When he received Pope Leo III in Paderborn, he wore a golden helmet. He wore a special sword decorated with precious stones only to receive foreign ambassadors and only twice in his life in Rome did he dress up as a Roman ruler with tunic, *chlamys* (a Greek cloak worn over battle armour) and Roman shoes. On festive occasions, however, he wore a gilded dress, shoes decorated with precious stones, a gold clasp on his cloak, and a diadem of gold covered with precious stones.

But Charlemagne also took a very active and personal interest in religion. He went to Mass every morning and attended the service at night as well. He collected manuals for prayer and joined in the responses of the daily office. Fast-days, however, he observed with bad grace, declaring that fasting was bad for his health. Only when he felt sick did he keep to a strict diet.

In spite of the fact that Charlemagne was a pious Christian, and meticulous in the observation of ecclesiastical prescriptions, he did not allow the prescriptions of canon law about marriage to influence his family life to any great extent. Indeed, the way in which he conducted his family affairs and presided over his family shows quite clearly that in his private life Charlemagne was still deeply immersed in the ancient tribal past of his ancestors. He himself was the son of one of his father's 'concubines', whom his father had 'married' several years after Charlemagne's birth. There were churchmen who considered this a blemish; but nobody else seems to have minded, least of all Charlemagne himself. The point was, of course, that in the eyes of ancient Frankish tradition there was no such thing as monogamy. A woman became a man's wife when he slept with her; and the children born of such a marriage were not considered bastards but were entitled to inherit. Although the transfer of power from the Merovingian House to Charlemagne's father

had been sanctioned and hallowed by the Church, Charlemagne felt deep down that that was not enough. Power and authority belonged to the whole clan and he did his best to extend his kinship bonds to the Merovingians by artificial means. His first two sons of a canonically recognised marriage were duly named after his grandfather and father, i.e. Charles and Pepin. But neither of the next two sons were named, as one would expect, after the patriarch of the family, Arnulf, even

Charlemagne and his second son, Pepin

though Arnulf was venerated as a saint. The next two sons were named Louis (=Clovis) and Lothair (=Chlothair), that is, after the names customary in the Merovingian family. In this way Charlemagne sought to bridge the gap and create an artificial bond of kinship in order to supplement the ecclesiastical justification of his kingship.

Charlemagne himself had five official wives. The first one, Himiltrude, was a Frankish girl and there was no canonically valid marriage. Early in his reign, when Charlemagne's mother was eager to form an alliance with the King of Lombardy, Himiltrude was sent away so that Charlemagne could marry a daughter of the King of Lombardy. When Charlemagne freed himself from his mother's tutelage and decided to invade the kingdom of Lombardy, he simply repudiated his second wife and married Hildegard, the daughter of a Swabian magnate. He seems to have been very happy with her: she bore him a large number of children, and during her lifetime he had no other wives. After her death he married Fastrada, for whom he had no great feelings. She seems to have been a cold and even cruel woman and long before her death Charlemagne took another wife, Liutgard. After Fastrada's death,

A musician playing the lute from the Lothair Psalter

he contracted a canonical marriage with Liutgard. When Liutgard died she was deeply mourned. Thereafter Charlemagne took a great many wives, four of whom are known to us: Gersuinda, Regina, Adallindis and Madelgarda. Some members of the clergy protested strongly against this obvious flouting of the Christian concept of marriage.

As was to be expected, Charlemagne had many sons and daughters. The eldest son was called Pepin and was destined for the succession. But when the third wife, Hildegard, gave birth to three more sons, Pepin was moved into the background. Perhaps it was because he was a hunchback, perhaps because Charlemagne was so fond of Hildegard. The second of these sons was finally baptized Pepin four years after his birth and, as a result of the favour showered upon these three new sons, the elder Pepin entered into a conspiracy with some discontented magnates. The conspiracy was betrayed and Pepin confined to a monastery. Eventually two of Hildegard's sons died and, just at the moment at which the elder Pepin might have become a dangerous rival to the last surviving son of Hildegard, he, too, died mysteriously. It was rumoured that he had not died a natural death. In the eyes of the Church, the elder Pepin was not a legitimate son and not entitled to inherit. But Charlemagne knew perfectly well that Church law was not very influential, that, according to ancient Frankish custom, all male children were entitled to inherit, and that, if Pepin survived, the sole succession of Louis, Hildegard's third son, would be in jeopardy.

In fact, if the convivial family atmosphere of the royal Court makes one think of Charlemagne as a kindly and jovial person, one must not overlook the fact that he also had a streak of really pagan brutality in him. There was not only the murder of Pepin. Two of his nephews who had taken refuge, together with their mother, with the King of Lombardy, were taken prisoner by Charlemagne and disappeared.

Charlemagne also had several daughters. He was inordinately fond of them and loved having them in his entourage. He did not like the idea of their marrying and departing from the royal household. He carried his fatherly love and desire to keep their company to what seems to us extraordinary lengths. He preferred them to have lovers rather than regular husbands as long as they kept residing within the circle of the family. His objection to their marriage had good reason. If these girls married and moved away with their husbands, their sons also, according to Frankish custom, would be entitled to inherit. Living away from the Court, Charlemagne rightly suspected that they might become centres of disaffection and intrigue and thus impair the unity of the kingdom. As long as they were living with him, even though they might take lovers, he could keep an eye on their offspring and gather them all in the firm circle of his clan.

Louis the Pious

Rotrud, after the end of her engagement to a Greek prince, had an 'illegitimate' son by Rorigon, Count of Le Mans, who grew up to be Abbot of St-Denys. Bertha, whom Charlemagne refused to allow to marry Offa, King of Mercia in Britain, was for many years the mistress of Angilbert, one of her father's trusted counsellors. One of her sons of this connection was Nithard, who became a learned historian. From his marriage to Fastrada Charlemagne had two more daughters, Theodrada and Hiltrud. They, too, never married but grew up to be abbesses—however, the lives they led were neither virginal nor abstemious in any other way.

There is no reason for thinking that the family life of the magnates differed in essentials. It was known that the Church taught monogamy and therefore distinguished between a wife and a concubine, a legitimate son and a bastard. But the whole matter was surrounded by uncertainties. The thoughtful cleric, if he consulted St Paul and read up his St Jerome and his St Augustine, would, on the whole, gain the impression that for a genuine Christian chastity was much the most desirable state to be in and he would think of marriage only as something second best. The average layman, on the other hand, no longer lived within the narrow confines of a tribal society and was therefore without any clear directives. Obviously he could not remain chaste and thus, as a Christian, was resigned to falling short of the ideal. For him the ancient directives were lacking and since the Church had not yet made up its mind whether the marriage ceremony was or was not a sacrament he lived suspended between the impossible ideal of chastity on one side and the sacramental

Reconstruction of the Palace of Ingelheim

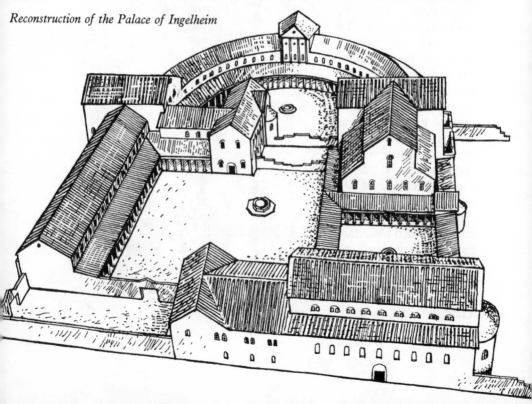

view of monogamous
and indissoluble
marriage on the other.
In this no-man's-land
there was a great deal
of freedom, and
Charlemagne's do-
mestic affairs were a
typical example of that
freedom.

Charlemagne's itin-
erant Court moved
from estate to estate.
On each of these villas
there was a palace,
some more elaborate
than others. But basi-
cally they were all
constructed according
to one pattern derived

Charlemagne's personal monogram

from Late Roman palaces. The palace at Ingelheim, for instance, was a
complex of buildings arranged round a large court. On one side there
was a festival hall leading to a smaller semicircular court at the other end
of which there was the church. In front of the church there was an
atrium with columns and opposite the church there was another great
hall. Palaces of this kind had been used by Charlemagne's Merovingian
predecessors, and the new and most spectacular palace which Charlemagne planned at Aix-la-Chapelle did not differ essentially from these
other palaces, except in size and splendour.

One of the most important parts of the palace was the church, the
chapel. It was named chapel after the 'capella sancti Martini', the cloak
of St Martin which was the most treasured relic in the possession of
Charlemagne's family. Special clerics became part of the Court retinue
in order to guard it. They were known as *capellani* (chaplains), and
eventually their duties extended to the care of the other relics as well.
The oratory in which they officiated was known as *capella* (chapel) after
the original relic. The presence of these chaplains afforded both Pepin

Model of Aix-la-Chapelle Palace (Leo Hugot)

and Charlemagne the first opportunity to have a real writing office at the palace, for these chaplains could be used as chancellors—they were able to write. And thus the guardianship of the cloak of St Martin proved the nucleus of a primitive administrative bureaucracy.

These royal chapels were heavily decorated. Altars often had a frontal of gold and silver. There were scores of vessels of gold and silver—covered with jewels—which were used in the celebration of the Mass; there were dozens of precious vestments, and on top of all this there were vast collections of precious relics. One gains the impression that the Christian mind of that age was wholly concerned with amassing costly and material objects of holy significance.

The most important of Charlemagne's palaces was Aix-la-Chapelle. This palace was to be a new Rome. The several parts of the palace were named after Roman buildings and were built according to ancient

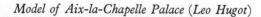

Model of Aix-la-Chapelle Palace (Leo Hugot)

Model of Aix-la-Chapelle Cathedral (Leo Hugot)

Roman and Byzantine models. The buildings were laid out as a square, with a triangle attached to it on the east side. The square was divided by a long, low, enclosed corridor which ran from south to north, and by a road which intersected it running from east to west at right angles. At the point of intersection there was a gateway with two smallish towers on the east side. On the first floor of that gateway there was the hall where Charlemagne used to sit in judgement. The layout cut across the net of roads of the ancient Roman spa; but Charlemagne had to build the chapel along an east–west axis and this axis determined the situation of the other buildings because, according to Roman prescription, everything had to be ordered as a square.

The main buildings were situated at the north and south end of the corridor. At the south end there was the royal chapel surrounded by a number of buildings for ecclesiastical purposes. The chapel was an octagon constructed on the model of the famous church of San Vitale in Ravenna. San Vitale had been built by the Emperor Justinian, and Charlemagne had it copied because it was a symbol of the Imperial tradition.

Inside, the chapel was subdivided into several floors. On the ground level there was the altar of Mary and on that level the servants assembled for divine service. On the first floor, which surrounded the inside of the octagon as a gallery, there was the royal throne, made of stone, and at the opposite end, the east side, the altar of Christ. The magnates would assemble in the gallery round the royal throne. On the highest level, there was the image of God, a golden mosaic which covered the ceiling of the cupola. It represented the fourth chapter of the Apocalypse, Christ enthroned among the 24 elders who had risen from their stools in order to offer their crowns to Him, and the four symbols of the Evangelists. In the centre there was a dove, the Holy Spirit, from which exuded rays of light breaking through a series of widening rings. The whole structure was an ideal emblem of the social structure of the kingdom. The servants at the bottom, when they looked up, saw themselves first surrounded by the magnates of the kingdom and, finally, enthroned above them, the figure of Christ in all His majesty.

On the other side of the square, at the north end, joined to the chapel by the long corridor, there was the royal hall. It was oblong, about 47 metres long and 20 metres wide.

The plan incorporated the ancient Roman baths. There were hot springs in Aix-la-Chapelle which had been used in ancient Roman times. The Roman baths had been destroyed in the fourth century, but Charlemagne now incorporated these springs into his palace and built a largish bath-house round them, approximately 28 by 15 metres.

The octagonal chapel, Aix-la-Chapelle Cathedral

When the plans for the palace at Aix-la-Chapelle were being drawn up, Charlemagne enjoyed a period of peace and comparative prosperity. He, therefore, wanted to build more than a royal palace: he intended to make Aix-la-Chapelle into a city on the model of ancient Rome. There was to be a forum and several other buildings. In deference to this plan, contemporaries even referred to the new building beside the chapel as 'the Lateran'. And the royal hall at the north end was designed on the model of the Roman basilica in Trier. From 795 onwards the palace at Aix-la-Chapelle became his permanent residence. There was easy access to the most important of his landed properties, there was good hunting in the forests, and there were hot springs; during the last 19 years of his life Charlemagne left Aix-la-Chapelle only rarely.

In order to provide worthy decorations for his capital he had several works of art from Italy transferred to Aix-la-Chapelle. Whole columns

Man with a hammer

and capitals were carried north and so was the equestrian bronze statue of Theodoric the Great. The removal of this heavy statue must have created great technical difficulties. But the desire to have it in Aix-la-Chapelle was not prompted solely by aesthetic considerations. Charlemagne considered Theodoric, the founder of one of the earliest Germanic kingdoms inside the ancient Roman Empire, as one of his precursors and wanted to create the impression that he was in fact one of his ancestors. The removal of the statue was, therefore, another instance of Charlemagne's desire to justify his authority by an artificial extension of his kin. There were also attempts to imitate Byzantine buildings to give the impression that the new capital of the Western Emperor was a powerful rival of the ceremonial centre of Eastern power. In the atrium of St

Peter's in Rome there was a large sculpture of a pine cone and Charlemagne had a somewhat smaller replica erected above the spring in the atrium of his own chapel. All in all, the whole construction was designed for representative purposes and was meant to give tangible and visible expression to the fact that a new form of political organisation was growing up in the place of the ancient Roman Empire and the not quite so ancient Byzantine Empire.

The domestic buildings where Charlemagne, his family, friends and entourage resided were much smaller and built mainly in wood. They were situated on the eastern side just in front of the royal hall and were connected both with the hall at the north end and the ecclesiastical buildings at the south end by a wooden corridor. The statue of Theodoric was erected in front of these wooden buildings, but faced the royal hall. The erection of these buildings drew a great many people to Aix-la-Chapelle, and during the last two decades of the reign there was feverish activity. Wagons arrived with the necessary stones and workshops were erected to create the works of art; masons and sculptors mingled with ordinary workers. Men were attracted from distant parts. But there was also forced labour and some foremen who were corrupt and lined their own pockets. If the original plan had been merely to build a symbol of Imperial power, the construction work soon attracted a vast number of people who became the nucleus of a real city.

Charlemagne's Court at Aix-la-Chapelle soon acquired fame. The King was generous and offered hospitality not only to scholars and artists but to pilgrims and ambassadors from foreign lands, and the general tone at Court was therefore extremely international and cosmopolitan. People came from England and Denmark, from the Balkans and from further east. They brought presents—relics, books, silks, tents and precious swords. In 796, after the country of the Avars in the Danube basin had been conquered, the loot was carried to Aix-la-Chapelle in 16 ox-wagons. In 802 there arrived a bizarre present from Harun al-Rashid, a white elephant. The elephant survived the hazardous journey across the Mediterranean and the Alps and died in 810. In 807 a Byzantine ambassador brought a tent, some incredibly beautiful hangings and curtains as well as two brass chandeliers and wonderful perfumes.

The colourful life which thus developed in Aix-la-Chapelle stood, however, in very marked contrast to the desolate poverty of culture in every other part of Charlemagne's dominions. With the exception of a few monks and a few leading ecclesiastics like Angilbert, Arno, Alcuin and Ebo, who had spent some time at the Court and then carried their culture to Abbeville, Salzburg, to Tours or to Reims, the rest of the population was not affected by the new style. The officials of the kingdom spoke and wrote a very simple and often grammatically crude Latin. The magnates probably spoke their own dialects and found that these Germanic dialects were sufficiently similar for them to understand one another. And when they met at the royal Court they began to

Charlemagne's throne in Aix-la-Chapelle Cathedral

designate that common language as *theodisk* (=*deutsch*, German). Charlemagne himself seems to have been aware that there existed a peculiar tension between the cultural amalgam of Roman, Byzantine and Arabic influences at his Court and the rustic and native coarseness of his magnates and the members of his own family. Towards the end of his life, when there was more peace and leisure, Charlemagne showed considerable interest in the native traditions of his own Germanic ancestors, which were fast being forgotten for lack of tribal life and also because of their pagan overtones. He suggested that someone write down the lays and songs of the ancient Franks and, according to his biographer Einhard, he decreed that in future the months of the year should be known not by their Roman names but by *theodisk*, i.e. vernacular, designations according to the agricultural activity or the climate or the holy day predominating in every month. January, for example, was to be called *Wintarmanoth*; April, *Ostarmanoth*; October, *Windumemanoth* and December, *Heilagmanoth*.

4 Government

Charlemagne's conception of the function of a ruler was basically primitive. This should not be taken in a derogatory sense. It simply means that Charlemagne saw himself as a tribal chieftain and, since he was a Christian, he derived much of his knowledge of human affairs from the Bible. The Bible was the most comprehensive history book with which he was acquainted—and much of it was filtered through the pages of St Augustine's *City of God*, which he knew well. He did not feel any close kinship with the Apostles or the Prophets; but he did see himself as a new David. He was the anointed of the Lord who held power over his tribesmen under God, and they owed obedience to him because he was to them what God was to all creatures. He modelled his conception of royal power on the Old Testament patriarchal rulers of the Children of Israel. As a result of this straightforward concept of power, Charlemagne held himself responsible for the welfare of his subjects in all respects. He would admonish the rich to be kind to the poor; he would supervise the weights and measures that were being used. He would control orthodoxy in religion, protect his subjects against foreign enemies, exhort his officials to be honest and just, and so forth. In this role as a patriarchal ruler he considered no limitations to his power. Although he was a chieftain, the ancient Frankish tribal institutions had been eroded sufficiently for the customary limitations on the chief's power to have been forgotten. So that at least in thought, if not in practice, the King's range of power extended to everything, including the Church. He presided over Church councils, dealt with bishops as he dealt with counts and markgraves and issued advice to the Pope.

The most tangible expression of this conception of his power is his legislative enterprise. The mere volume of his legislation is unique in medieval history. The large number of his written laws and instructions which have come down to us comprise no less than 1,075 separate pieces of 'legislation'. They were collected and issued in bundles known as 'capitularies'. Each capitulary consisted of a series of admonitions, rules, regulations and orders concerning all things under the sun. They touched on private manners, on economics and trade, on religion and justice and warfare. Some are addressed to specific officials; others are couched in general tones. Nothing was too big or too small to escape the King's attention, and these capitularies, if nothing else, bear witness to his constant vigilance. They were not formally enacted by a legislative

Part of a Carolingian diploma, showing Charlemagne's signature

body. They were issued on the King's authority as an expression of his concern and responsibility for the welfare of the people entrusted to him by God. Charlemagne was unique among medieval rulers in his scrupulous concern for the welfare of his subjects.

Charlemagne realised that there was no point in displaying such

A ruler, from the Martyrologium of Wandalbert of Prüm

legislative activity unless there existed at least a rudimentary administrative system. He could not be in all places in his vast dominions at the same time and, therefore, he elaborated the custom practised for three centuries by his predecessors of delegating royal authority to counts. These counts were supposed to be officials who represented the King in a circumscribed number of counties. It is estimated that, if the whole area of the kingdom had been covered with counties, there would have been between 250 and 300 counts at any one time—although the sources mention no more than 120 for the whole of the reign. In fact, the subdivision into counties was far from complete; and there were probably many magnates who called themselves counts without any distinct authority to do so. The counts were to hold courts of justice at regular intervals, levy an army when the King required one, and collect the contributions which were due to the Crown. They were supposed to visit the King once a year in order to keep in touch. When Charlemagne had a free hand, he preferred to appoint men to such office from among the Frankish magnates of that region between the Rhine, Meuse and Moselle where his power and holdings were strongest. But, for the most part, he had no

free hand and his wish to retain control
over these officials remained unfulfilled.

To begin with, a count could be rewarded for his services only by a grant
of land. Charlemagne was unable to pay
a salary. But a grant of land meant that
the count and his family would become
solidly established on it, and that on the
count's death his sons would expect to
inherit it. Charlemagne, like his predecessors, had no chance of depriving the
count's heirs of the land and so it was
usually the way of least resistance to let
them keep it and allow them to succeed
to their father's office. In many cases
this led to the succession of incompetent
and dishonest counts, though not necessarily so. But in all cases it led to an
ever-growing weakening of royal authority. There was great tension between
the patriarchal conception of rulership
and the idea that, owing to the vastness
of the territory, power had to be delegated. And there was further tension
between the idea of central royal power
capable of delegation to appointed
officials and the brute fact that such
power could be 'delegated' only to landed
magnates (who exercised it anyway).

*A Frankish count. From
the frescoes in St Benedetto,
Malles*

The greatest difficulty in keeping the counts in a subordinate position
as royal agents arose from the nature of the society itself. If the King
appointed an indigenous magnate to the countship in a certain district,
he could at least be certain that that magnate would enjoy the co-
operation of the other magnates in the region, most of whom were
probably related to him. In such a case the King could indirectly avail
himself of the social allegiances and cohesiveness of the region. But this
arrangement also meant that the appointed count would be closely

identified with the interests of the local magnates and would not therefore be likely to represent the King's interests or to protect orphans, widows and the poor against the other magnates. If, on the other hand, the King sent a stranger into the district as a count, he would not get any co-operation from the local families. Such a stranger might be a more loyal servant than a local magnate; but he would also have no machinery to work through and his authority, in spite of the best intentions, was bound to remain very small. Furthermore, being a stranger in the district, he would not be restrained by indigenous sanctions or local family obligations and might thus be tempted to become an exploiter and oppressor not only of the poor and helpless but also of the local magnates, whom he might even turn against the King as a result of his unrestrained behaviour. Or, again, in newly conquered territories some native leaders might be willing to become the King's counts and co-operate with the conqueror. But, in such cases, they tended to become estranged from their own people and consequently

Bronze folding chair of a Carolingian ruler, the so-called Dagobert throne

Reliquary of an arm of Charlemagne

lost influence and authority, and then they were of comparatively little use to Charlemagne. If and when their older ties began to reassert themselves, moreover, their function as representatives of central authority would be impaired. Last, but not least, a count could not easily keep his own property in the region permanently separate from the lands he was invested with as a reward for his office. Even if he was personally able to resist the temptation to fuse the two, he was under constant pressure from his family to do so. And if he resisted *that* pressure, he weakened his standing in the region and was, therefore, less useful to the King. Slowly, in each county, the royal lands became the count's lands. Thus royal authority was weakened. And where this did *not* happen, royal authority was weak anyway because the count either already was or became alienated from the other magnates to whom he was related. In short, in spite of the constant flood of admonitions and instructions issued to counts, it was a situation in which the King was bound to lose. The King's real and effective power depended on the voluntary co-operation of the landed magnates who considered it their common interest to owe allegiance. The count as a royal official could play only a very minor role in keeping the vast dominions together.

Apart from levying an army, the count's most important function in every district was supposed to be the administration of justice, that is the suppression of wanton fighting and the termination of feuds. The procedures to be followed in order to achieve those aims were laid down in minute detail. There was to be at least one court of law in every county, the *mallus*, which was to be presided over by the count or by an official appointed by him. The main function of the tribunal was to find the law: there were several assessors, reliable men from the neighbourhood of the place where the offence was committed, whose task was to declare what the customary punishment for the offence was. These assessors were selected by the count and were known as *rachinburgi*. In 780, the King issued a directive that henceforth the assessors were to be permanent members of the court (and nominated by it) so that they could evolve some grasp of legal principles through experience. They now became known as *scabini*. In Italy, the *scabini* may well have been semi-professional lawyers, but north of the Alps no such 'lawyers' were available. The result was that the King's order empowered the count to appoint a small number of local magnates to the court and thus deprive the assembly of freemen of much power. These *scabini*, far from adding a professional element to the court, merely served to turn it into an instrument of power for the local magnates. The *mallus* was originally a popular institution—an assembly of the freemen of the district. Charlemagne wanted to place this indigenous method of administering justice under his protection and therefore ordered the counts, as representatives of the King, to preside. But the counts, unless they had a personal interest in the case before the *mallus*, could see no urgent reason why they should take charge of a folk custom. When they were able to exclude the freemen, on the other hand, they had an incentive for presiding.

The hearing was opened by the plaintiff stating his case. The assessors then found the law and laid down what methods were to be employed to discover whether the accused was guilty or innocent. These methods always amounted to an ordeal or a judgement of God. Accused and plaintiff might be ordered to settle the question of guilt by a judicial duel. If this was the case, the actual fighting might be done not by the two parties but by their 'champions'. Alternatively, the assessors might order that one of the two parties should hold a hot iron or immerse their hands in boiling water. The truth of their allegation was determined according to the time it took for the injuries thus incurred to heal. And again, the assessors could demand a trial by oath. This meant that both parties had to take an oath on the truth of their allegations and provide a fixed number of oath-helpers, friends or relatives who would be prepared to support the oath by one of their own.

In practice, this administration of justice left very much to be desired. It was extremely difficult to insist on the counts' duty to hold regular courts of law according to the prescribed rules. Whenever a case came up in which the count or a member of his family or a friend or relative in the district was involved, the count would prefer to use means of his own to bring it to what he considered a successful conclusion. The lower classes were almost always helpless, especially when they were vassals of some lord. In many cases, the counts preferred their own pleasures and

Charlemagne

pastimes to the burdens of their office (like the King himself, they were passionately addicted to hunting), and the courts were neglected. All in all, especially in the more outlying districts of the kingdom, royal authority as delegated to the count meant very little, and people settled their quarrels and disputes according to their own traditional and indigenous method, the feud.

When a person had been injured in life or limb or property, some members of his clan would gather and inflict a comparable injury on the offender or a member of his family or clan. The other clan might then retaliate by inflicting yet another injury upon a member of the clan of the initial victim—and so forth. This system of judicial vengeance was very old. It was efficient in a society in which there was no central authority capable of keeping the peace and it embodied some diffuse guarantee of security by the principle of collective responsibility. The members of a family were likely to keep a close eye on one another lest an attack on a member of another clan unleash that clan's vengeance on the original clan. The one great disadvantage of the system was the fact that at least in theory there was no end to such vengeances: they could be carried on for generations. A long time before the age of Charlemagne, Kings had promoted the evolution of a fixed tariff according to which such feuds could be settled. If compensation was made for the initial injury, the need for further vengeance was obviated. The compensation was known as the *wergild* and it differed according to the social status of the injured person. In the age of Charlemagne there was very strong pressure on people to submit their feuds to the *mallus*, which would assess the *wergild* and hand over two-thirds of it to the injured man or his family—the other third went to the King. But the King could not hope to abolish the feud altogether, because neither his power nor that of his delegates, the counts, was strong enough to provide a viable alternative. Apart from the administration of justice, the count was also supposed to protect all those who could not well protect themselves, i.e. widows and orphans, monks and clergy, and to keep an eye on the stewards of royal estates situated in his territory. All these duties offered further temptations. If the county was situated on the borders of the kingdom, the counts were also responsible for defence and, in such cases, they were given special titles and larger estates in order to cope with such tasks.

Coin showing the head of Charlemagne

The counts had to be recruited from among the ranks of the magnates, and they exhibited all the callousness and brutal aggressiveness and acquisitive instincts of that class of men. The royal office did not mean so much a special responsibility as a special opportunity for indulging those instincts and appetites. In fact, the very forces making for loyalty to the King depended on the King's willingness to sanction these appetites by the grant of an office, so that the very cohesion of the kingdom depended on the gradual dismemberment of centralised power. Not that it had ever been centralised. But the magnates looked to the King and recognised him *because* he kept authorising the office which enabled them to advance their fortunes as magnates. One might almost say that this authority was proportional to the degree to which he used it to sanction their behaviour. With the growth of their landed property, these men had fast lost their tribal status and had thus become exempt from the moral sanction which a closely knit tribal status would have entailed. On the other side, there was next to nothing to make up for this

Christ and the four Evangelists

loss and to instil a higher morality or a sense of public obligation. The King issued decree after decree inveighing against corruption and bribery. The most dire punishments were threatened if counts accepted presents and neglected their duties. All in vain. Even those exceptional magnates who sought instruction in the precepts of Christian morality could not easily obtain it. Alcuin mentioned that a count had approached him for moral advice, but reported that it had been impossible to arrange a meeting. Alcuin therefore sent written advice—but it consisted of nothing but commonplace admonitions of the most vague kind. Indeed, the prevailing social climate made most people think that religious precepts were for the clergy only and that the commands of the Bible applied only to monks. The moral ideals to which men did pay lip-service were derived not from ascetic Christianity but from the more ancient precepts of pagan morality. It was held that a man ought to be

A Frankish King and his officials. Count Vivian's Bible, Tours

generous towards the Church and protect those of his dependants who could not bear arms. He had to show friendship to men of his own rank and to the clergy provided they were of high birth. He had to have courage and valour in warfare and display a great deal of ingenuity. There was nothing in all this which might prevail upon a member of the upper classes to subordinate his own interests to those of the public he was meant to 'serve' and to take the place of the ancient efficient sanctions and pressures which would have placed a restraint on his instincts and appetites.

The King was well aware of the powerful centrifugal tendencies and the vast amount of corruption and aggressiveness and dishonesty which dominated this scheme of government. In order to counteract them, he tried to strengthen the central seat of government. Apart from appointing the conventional officers of the palace, a constable, a cellarer, a marshal, a chamberlain, and a custodian of the gate, Charlemagne gave special prominence to the count palatine and to the chancellor.

The count palatine was a lay magnate, specially devoted to the King and he acted as a permanent president of a special tribunal which sat in the royal palace. The assessors were always persons of high rank and, when the King was presiding in person, the count palatine acted as the chief assessor. The procedure was less formal than that of the *mallus*, for the assessor was not bound to observe the local custom of any one region and was therefore able to allow himself to be guided by his wisdom and his sense of equity. It is noteworthy that on at least one occasion we find the Roland who was to become the centre of so many Carolingian legends among the counts acting as assessors at the royal tribunal.

The other chief officer of the palace was the chancellor. Unlike the count palatine, he had to be an ecclesiastic, preferably a bishop. In order to secure good men for this position, Charlemagne obtained in 794 a special ruling from the Pope to allow bishops to reside away from their diocese. The chancellor presided over the royal chancellery, the writing office, and was often the same man as the royal chaplain, who was the head of the palace clergy in charge of the royal chapel.

Charlemagne was anything but naïve. He knew very well that, as things were, he had 'fewer supporters than subverters of justice' in his service. He realised that the strengthening of the palace administration would have no effect unless it could be made to have repercussions in local administration. He therefore instituted a system of special royal messengers, *missi dominici*. This institution reproduced the co-operation between a lay magnate and an ecclesiastic on the local level. The whole kingdom was divided into a number of districts, each including several counties. Each district was to be visited once a year by two perambulating *missi*, one lay and the other clerical. At the end of their circuit they were to report to the King in person. Their chief task was to supervise the counts and the counts were to support them in every county until all complaints against the counts had been heard or dealt with. They were to announce their impending arrival by letters to the count and invite all people in the county to come forward with complaints. In order to minimise the possibility of corruption, magnates appointed as royal envoys were always assigned to a district in which they themselves held neither office nor land. Only very specially trusted servants and friends like Archbishop Arno of Salzburg or Abbot Fardulf of St Denys were entrusted with the authority of *missi* in the region in which they resided and officiated.

But here, too, circumstances militated against Charlemagne's intentions. These envoys, like everybody else of note, belonged to the upper classes and were prey to their own rapaciousness. There was great temptation for them to accept bribes and presents on arrival in a county; and, even when they were honest enough not to succumb to temptation, they had little power of action against a count whom they might find guilty of maladministration. Alcuin did not think it amiss to warn his own friend, Arno, a man of well-known integrity, that he ought not to accept bribes in matters of justice; and Theodulf, another worthy cleric, wrote that when he was a *missus* he had been flooded with bribes, ranging from precious works of art to very modest articles such as a pair of boots.

The whole class of magnates, even if they were often at each other's throats, exhibited a certain kind of solidarity and co-operation based on their community of interests, which were always the enlargement of their landed holdings and the advancement of their worldly fortunes. 'If I am ever charged in the palace with a crime', one of them wrote, 'I shall have my advocates there. I shall find a large number of relatives and friends who will see to it that the King's wrath will not fall upon me.' In principle, such communities of interests among the ruling classes are operative in all societies. But, in the age of Charlemagne, there was next to nothing to counter such communities effectively.

There was, for instance, the notorious case of the unfortunate Italian widow. A man of high official rank had been supposed to administer her property. But he had broken his trust and taken over the property for himself. The widow complained to the King, who ordered an inquiry. However, owing to the combined efforts of a large number of both lay and ecclesiastical officials, the inquiry petered out. Eventually, the poor widow journeyed to Aix-la-Chapelle to seek justice and on her arrival Wala, Charlemagne's cousin, was put in charge of her case. But in spite of the best of intentions he could make no headway. The accused hired assassins who murdered the widow and, to cover up, he paid one of the three assassins to murder the remaining two: '. . . the whole of Italy and its officials, corrupted by bribes, was busily intriguing to make sure that he who was known to all as a rapacious murderer, should not be found guilty. . . . In fact all the most influential persons in the royal palace endeavoured to produce witnesses and all manner of subterfuges in order to secure the acquittal of a guilty man.'

5   The Army

The most tangible aspect of Charlemagne's power was the army. According to ancient tradition, the King was entitled to demand military service from all freemen of the tribe. Charlemagne never completely gave up his right to demand military service from all freemen; but, as we shall see, for practical purposes it did not amount to much. The armies he led consisted instead of an almost professional class of warriors, whose members were all rich landowners or the vassals of rich landowners.

When the King wanted to go to war, he issued orders to counts, bishops and abbots throughout the realm to meet him, together with their armed men, at an appointed place. According to very old tribal custom, the King would meet the freemen of the tribe at a general assembly in March or May, deliberate with them and then depart on a military campaign. In the age of Charlemagne nothing much was left of this custom except that the general assembly was still the time and place for the meeting of the King's warriors. It was not so much that the army assembled because the meeting was held, but that the meeting was held because the army had to assemble. When the men were assembled, Charlemagne used the assembly to communicate his plans to his men— so that there was little left of the deliberative character of the ancient tribal meeting. The occasion of the assembly of such a large number of people was also used at times to find out what was going on in the kingdom. 'Why', Charlemagne would, for example, demand to know, 'is it that so many vassals who run away from their lords are welcomed by other magnates?' And on another occasion he wanted to know why so many pastors of souls failed to set a good example.

Even so, the assembly of the army was the occasion on which Charlemagne could get in touch personally with many magnates, lay as well as ecclesiastical. As the army was assembling, he often held separate meetings with the most notable of the magnates in a quiet near-by place, the results of which would eventually be announced formally to all the assembled men. The King would then be seen walking up and down

Battle scenes. Utrecht Psalter

among the assembled men, exchanging words with them and boosting their morale by his presence. His personal presence among his men and their expression of their loyalty and co-operation was taken as their approval of his policies. The general assembly, therefore, although it was summoned for a purely military purpose and although it bore only a vague resemblance to the original tribal meeting, served a social and a political purpose. Towards the end of the reign, Charlemagne further rationalised this ancient habit of meeting his magnates and summoned smaller assemblies to his favourite palaces in Aix-la-Chapelle or Heristal, specifically for talks rather than for military campaigns; the result of such consultation was usually embodied in important capitularies.

The assembly also served as a ritual occasion, although as a result of the official espousal of Christianity, nobody clearly mentioned the residues of tribal ritual which, no doubt, were present. But we have an inkling of the ritual purpose of the assembly because, no matter at what time of the year it was held for the sake of military convenience, it was always referred to as the *magis campus* or the *campus madius*, i.e. the field of May—thus reminding the participants of the ancient, pre-Christian seasonal ritual on which it had originally been based.

One of the chief duties of the count was to raise an army in his county. He was supposed to lead the contingent in person to meet the King. A refusal to obey the count's orders could be punished by a fine of 60 *solidi*—an enormous sum by the standards of the time and so large that most people in the county could never hope to pay it. But a man who deserted from a campaign was to forfeit his property and lose his life. It was realised, however, that a refusal to render military service was not necessarily due to malice. There were many people in the county who were too poor to find the necessary equipment, and for this reason the King issued very detailed regulations to define the kind of contribution which could reasonably be expected of them. It was directed that, if there were four men with small holdings, one of the four was to be equipped by a common contribution, and the other three allowed to stay at home. For the most part, not even four small holdings would be sufficient to equip one soldier, and in practice the four men would merely send some supplies to the count, who would use these supplies to equip one of his own vassals. According to another directive it was laid down that those who had five pounds' worth of chattels had to pay the full fine for refusing to serve. Those who owned three pounds' worth had to pay 30 *solidi*; those with two pounds, 10 *solidi*; and those with one pound, only 5 *solidi*. But in no case were the wife and children of the man to be deprived of their garments. Legally and officially there was thus a great deal of flexibility. But in practice the system provided the counts with innumerable opportunities for extortion and protection rackets.

As a result, the contingents raised by the county were always very small. A count often did not manage to provide more than 100 warriors from a county of as many as 50,000 inhabitants. But counts were not even anxious to try their best to raise as many men as

Sword traditionally associated with Charlemagne

possible. When the order to raise men arrived, they first of all preferred to use it as an opportunity to make extraordinarily great demands
on as many people as possible—hoping that men would prefer to commend themselves and their holdings to the count or to members of his
family in the county in order to avoid military service. The count was
not always a loyal servant of the King, and was tempted to use royal
orders as a pretext for advancing his own power and wealth.

Military service was indeed a very costly burden. Ever since the days
when Charles Martel, early in the eighth century, had organised an
army to resist the Moorish advance into Gaul, the main body of the
army had been the cavalry. The standard equipment for a horseman
consisted of the following pieces, worth a fortune in cows:

a helmet, 6 cows
a tunic or vest covered with metal plates, 12 cows

Man with bow and arrow

sword and sheath, 7 cows
armour leggings, 6 cows
lance and shield, 2 cows
the horse, 12 cows.

The full equipment, therefore,
would amount to the equivalent
of 45 cows, which was a very considerable fortune in livestock and
very much more than all but the
wealthiest could afford. If we look
at the figures for the wealthiest
royal estates in northern Gaul, we
find that there were only 50 cows in
Annappes, 30 in Vitry, six in Cyso-
ing and six in Somain—not counting
oxen, heifers or bullocks. A cow was
probably worth one *solidus*, so that
the fine for not obeying the
summons to military service was
very much greater than the cost
of even the fullest equipment.

Warfare. Utrecht Psalter

The most expensive pieces of equipment, apart from the horse itself, were those which were made of metal. By comparison, the lance and the shield, made of wood and leather respectively, were cheap. But, even if it was cheaper to serve than to pay the fine, the cost of the equipment was still prohibitive to all but a few. By comparison with the stiff fine for an outright refusal, there was only a nominal punishment for late arrival at the appointed place: the culprit had to abstain from wine and meat for as many days as he had been late. Obviously, delays were common and the conditions of the roads and the difficulties of communication frequently frustrated the best intentions.

Many warriors were also equipped with bow and arrows. But a bow, to be effective, had to be well made; and, because of the poor standard of craftsmanship, bows were hard to come by. On one occasion a special warning was issued that men were not to present themselves with sticks in place of the bow. Archery, of course, required special skill. And if it was difficult to find good archers, it was even more difficult to make effective use of a bow on a horse. A man on horseback, carrying a lance and a shield, had to have considerable training to be able to handle a bow effectively: for what was he to do with the shield when taking aim with the bow? And as he was aiming the bow the shield would not afford much protection, since it was dangling from an arm.

The most common weapons were the lance, the sword and the axe. The lance was the most popular of all. The most common form of lance had a longish iron blade with a cross-bar at the end to prevent too deep a penetration. Other blades had a counter-hook. The axe was used for throwing and the most widely used kind had a curved blade and a curved stick. It was alleged that it behaved like a boomerang: if it missed its target, it described a circle and returned to the hands of its owner. The sword was very different from the Roman sword which was used for stabbing and piercing. The Frankish sword was a *spatha*, a longish sword with a short handle. It was worn in a sheath, and both handle and sheath were covered with precious stones. It was an expensive weapon, frequently worn for show and more widely used by the magnates. The common man used a simpler sword, the so-called *scramasax*. It had a very long handle and a broad blade. It was held with both hands and wielded like a club. There was a short model with a blade 30 centimetres long and a long one with a 60-centimetre blade.

The most effective form of protection was the shield. The shield was either round or oval. It was made of hardened leather and painted in garish colours. In the centre it had a hardened cone with a sharp point. Apart from the shield, those who could afford it wore a tunic or vest covered with small metal plates. This garment was extremely expensive, and therefore rare. Slightly less rare was the helmet. Like the sword, it was derived from ancient Germanic and Asian head gear. It consisted of a metal ring on which strips of metal were mounted which met at the top. The spaces between the strips were filled by metal plates. Two further plates dangled from the ring to protect the cheeks. Ring and plates were often decorated and at the very top there was a small hook for fixing a sort of

Drawing of two Frankish warriors, showing the weapons they used and the clothes of the period

plume. None of the plumes worn have been preserved and we do not, therefore, know what they looked like. In Lombardy warriors frequently wore a cross instead of the plume.

Foot soldiers, on the whole, were beginning to prove less effective and mounted warriors were becoming more and more important. But since horses were hard to come by (the above-mentioned royal

Carolingian infantry

estates had only 51, 79, 44 and 30 mares each) the need for cavalry further limited the number of people who could render effective military service. In 761 one Isanhard sold his ancestral property and a slave to the monks of St Gall for a horse and a sword. Moreover, a mounted warrior became a formidable fighter only with the introduction of stirrups. Without stirrups, every time he lashed out with his sword or was pushed by someone's spear he was likely to lose control. Only when he could keep himself firmly in his stirrups could he add the horse's momentum to his thrust. But, although stirrups seem to have been introduced into Gaul during the eighth century, there is no clear sign that the Frankish cavalry became a very formidable fighting force. The adoption of the stirrup helped to promote the fortunes of the mounted warrior; but it took a very considerable time before there appeared any revolutionary change in fighting habits.

There was no training and no drill. The only sign of proper military organisation was the head of an animal, which was carried on a spear in front of the army as it was marching along. The animal's head was wide open and a hose of sacking was fixed to the back to allow the wind to blow through. If we are to judge from one ninth-century drawing, they used to put burning oil into the animal's mouth. The small flame would serve as a signal at night and the hot air, escaping into the hose at the back, would cause that hose to rise horizontally and move in the air.

The army was an amorphous body with very little discipline and very ill-equipped for systematic fighting. There were constant problems of discipline. People not only joined late and left without permission; there was also a great deal of drunkenness. Not that the punishments were harsh: warriors found drunk were to drink nothing but water until they had reformed. During the whole long reign of Charlemagne only two genuine battles were fought—and even these battles were of no decisive significance. At the battle near the Süntel Mountains in Saxony, Charlemagne's men 'took their weapons and advanced not in order to attack the enemy ranged in battle formation, but in order to pursue the enemy who were in full flight'. The entire military success of Charlemagne depended on the fact that his opponents were even less capable of putting a proper army into the field. Contemporaries were strangely aware of the fact that Charlemagne kept winning wars without much real fighting. They piously explained these curious victories by the massiveness of prayers and fasts which had preceded the battles in question or, as in the case of the war against the Lombards, by the intervention of St Peter.

The army was not only amorphous; it was also very small. It rarely consisted of more than 5,000 fighting men. Given the fact that in any one district only a few men could be summoned effectively for military service, it became necessary to summon soldiers from very far away. Bavarians fought in Aquitaine, Alamans from Swabia in Spain; Frisians fought against the Avars in the Danube region and Burgundians fought in Bohemia. On one occasion, when Charlemagne learnt on his return from a campaign in Spain that the Saxons had invaded the Rhineland, an effective defence could only be organised by the despatch of members of his own army. There were not enough fighting men available in the immediate neighbourhood of the invaded country to offer resistance.

The bulk of the army consisted of horsemen. But their numbers were swelled by a sizeable group of servants and coachmen who were in attendance on the real warriors. These men, though armed in a very primitive way and probably lacking the standards of valour and bravery upheld by the professional warriors, were always a welcome addition to the fighting force of the army.

Since it was necessary to summon men from distant regions, elaborate provisions had to be made for the supply of food. And this in turn created problems of transport. In order to avoid glaring injustice, it was laid down that men summoned for an expedition to Spain from north of the Loire were allowed to count their prescribed term of military service (i.e. three months) from the time they crossed the Loire; while men who lived south of the Loire were to count their military service from the time they reached the Pyrenees. Similarly, for an expedition against the Slavs, people were to count their service from the

Carolingian cavalry from the Golden Psalter, St Gall

time they crossed the Rhine if they came from Gaul; and from the time they crossed the Elbe if they lived in Saxony. But, given the slow travelling time and the difficulties of transport, three months was not a long period. And this limitation of time again greatly diminished the fighting efficiency of these armies.

But the greatest problem was the problem of food. As a rule each warrior had to bring enough food to last for the whole campaign. In some cases it was laid down that he had to bring enough food for three months, and enough clothing and weapons to last for six months. This meant that he had to bring a wagonload, because a horse could not carry enough. On the whole, there had to be one wagon for every warrior; and even then the whole army had to be accompanied by a herd of cattle which were slaughtered for food. The wagons were sturdy and had to be protected by a leather cover. They were supposed to be stocked with a shield, a lance, bow and arrows, for the defence of the load, if necessary. Moreover, the special equipment for a siege had to be carried in the wagons. There were axes and hatchets, crow-bars and slings—all things which added considerably to the load. Each wagon was supposed to carry 12 measures of flour or 12 measures of wine. But the wagons and the herd of cattle only provided the barest essentials.

Since most of the warriors were magnates, they were not content with the barest essentials. They had to have servants and food for the servants and they were in the habit of carrying with them a large amount of drink, that is, both wine and beer. And since there was no end to the goods which the warriors might require, an army of that kind also attracted a crowd of pedlars, entertainers and, last but not least, women. All in all, the wagon train and herds, the servants and other people made up an army which was very much larger than the body of warriors. An army of this kind could move only slowly and with difficulty. The roads were very bad and the construction of the wagons was exceedingly primitive. Each wagon was drawn by two oxen. But since there were no wheel-bearings, progress was slow and a wagon could not carry much. Oxen were also notoriously slow and, though their traction power was as great as that of horses, the latter were preferable because they could move faster and therefore pull a wagon a greater distance for the same amount of fodder. But while the ancient method of yoking oxen was quite efficient, the ancient method of harnessing horses was not. The Romans had harnessed horses by fastening a narrow strap round its neck. On the least exertion the strap started to strangle the horse, so that it could barely pull as light a load as four hundredweight. In the age of Charlemagne the infinitely more efficient method of harnessing horses which is still in use was beginning to be introduced. But the new method spread slowly and here again, as in the case of the new plough, the three-field rotation system and the stirrup we find that a technological invention by itself, when not accompanied by suitable social and cultural conditions, could not bring about any very revolutionary changes.

Warriors. Utrecht Psalter

In order to make up for these unwieldy and inefficient fighting forces, Charlemagne also kept a very small watch in his own palaces. It consisted of a number of young men who

A wagon drawn by two horses in harness

were supposed to be unmarried and unattached to the land. They lived with him in his palaces and were fed and supplied, on active service, directly from the royal domains. This palace guard was part of the royal household and, correspondingly, very efficient. They travelled with the King and their presence and support increased the King's need to keep moving himself from palace to palace to make sure that he would have adequate supplies of food for his very large household. In order to facilitate their employment for active service, Charlemagne established special manors in those parts of the royal domain where there were no palaces. The tenants were supposed to make their contribution to these manors so that the royal guard could provision themselves. These special manors also enabled the guard to be more mobile than the ordinary army which had to carry its own food.

6   The Church

The Church had been established both in Gaul and in the Rhineland long before the Frankish conquests. But in the Rhineland it had suffered a sharp decline with the disappearance of the Roman legions. Only the barest traces had remained in some of the rapidly vanishing towns. In Gaul it had continued to flourish south of the Loire under its bishops, abbots and saints until there, too, the decline of city life set in during the seventh century. With the decline of city life there declined not only the communities of the faithful, but also the importance of the bishops who had been elected by the clergy and the citizens to preside over them. Bishops continued to hold office; but more and more they had to rely on grants of land for their income. And, as the economic basis of their lives shifted to the land they held, they became for all practical purposes indistinguishable from the ordinary large landowners. There was a very rapid decline in their educational standards and their interest in theology and an equally rapid decline in their interest in their pastoral work. The bishops became instead an integral part of the land-owning classes and adjusted their lives accordingly. And, as the bishoprics ceased to be civic and became rural institutions, they became coveted possessions of the wealthy and important families in the district.

With the absence of clerical standards, bishops would continue to lead the kind of life they had been accustomed to lead in the bosoms of their families. They engaged in blood-feuds, they went hunting, they rendered the king the military service which he expected from other magnates, they kept women and ceased to wear clerical garments. Their palaces became centres of secular life: they held banquets and entertained jugglers and mimes and minstrels. As they became absorbed into the class of landed magnates, they not only lost their interest in Church affairs, but also pursued their acquisitive appetites with full vigour. They used the last remnants of their 'spiritual' authority in order to force the poor to surrender their holdings to them, either by promising eternal salvation or by threatening eternal damnation. If these methods did not yield the desired results, they resorted to violence in order to make small landowners surrender their property. They exploited those who were unable to resist like any secular magnate; they bribed people to give false testimony in their favour. And, like secular magnates, they sought to make the episcopal lands hereditary in their families. There were veritable episcopal dynasties where the episcopal office and the holdings were passed from father to son for several generations.

The land-owning bishop was subject to the same local pressures as the secular official. A bishop, to be effective, had to be appointed from among the local magnates. But, if he belonged to one of the local families, he would endeavour during the tenure of his office to merge his episcopal lands with those of his family to make sure that his successor, if he belonged to another family, would be able to recover as little as possible.

The consequences of these pressures for the observance and propagation of religion were disastrous. There was little enough incentive to understand the deeper meaning of Christianity, and pagan cults and beliefs and hundreds of extravagant superstitions flourished among the population. The bishops, who had become indistinguishable from the land-owning magnates, had neither the interest nor ability to pursue their pastoral duties. Even the most elementary ritual came to be neglected and often enough the peasants found it difficult to have their children baptized or to obtain extreme unction before their death. All this produced the worst possible effect on public and private morality: the ancient religion and its ritual had disappeared as an effective system of communal worship and the new religion, owing to the social and economic condition of its guardians, was not able to become a substitute. The elimination of the old religion had been brought about by missionaries. Either a King and his whole band of warriors had been

Musicians playing the lyre, horn and organ

Baptism

converted or smaller peasant communities had been won over. The words and instructions of missionaries would have remained with out much force if at the same time the migration and the growth of the large landed estate had not eroded the communal institutions of the old religion. On the landed estate and its manors, there was no opportunity for continuing the old tribal ritual and only its superstitions continued to flourish. But at the same time the institutions of the new religion were linked to city life. Where they became assimilated to and absorbed by the landed estate, they ceased to function.

In those parts of the dominions of Charlemagne in which the Christian religion had only just been introduced in the generation preceding his reign, and in those districts like Saxony where it was being introduced during his own reign, the situation was slightly different. The economic basis of the bishoprics was very similar to that of the bishops of Gaul. The new bishoprics too were based on land and the new bishops were, above all, landowners. There were no cities as yet, no clergy and no people who could elect their pastors. But, just because these bishoprics were new and had been founded in order to promote the conversion of the heathen, the first appointees were often men of considerable quality who accepted their appointment because of a religious vocation. For this reason, bishoprics like Salzburg, Mainz, Paderborn, and Münster were held during the reign of Charlemagne by men of exemplary conduct.

During the generation preceding Charlemagne, a reform movement had been instituted. Under the inspiration of Boniface, who had come from Britain in order to convert the Germans to Christianity, it was decreed for the whole of the Frankish realm that certain minimum standards of episcopal behaviour were to be observed. These standards were not very exacting by comparison with modern ideas; but at the time they presented a very formidable programme of ecclesiastical reform. The clergy, high and low, were to refrain from hunting and from carrying arms. If they accompanied military expeditions, they were to do so only in order to say Mass and guard relics. The clergy were to dress themselves in clerical garments and were not allowed to keep

Genesis scenes from the Moutier-Grandval Bible—from the conception of Adam and Eve to their expulsion from the Garden of Eden

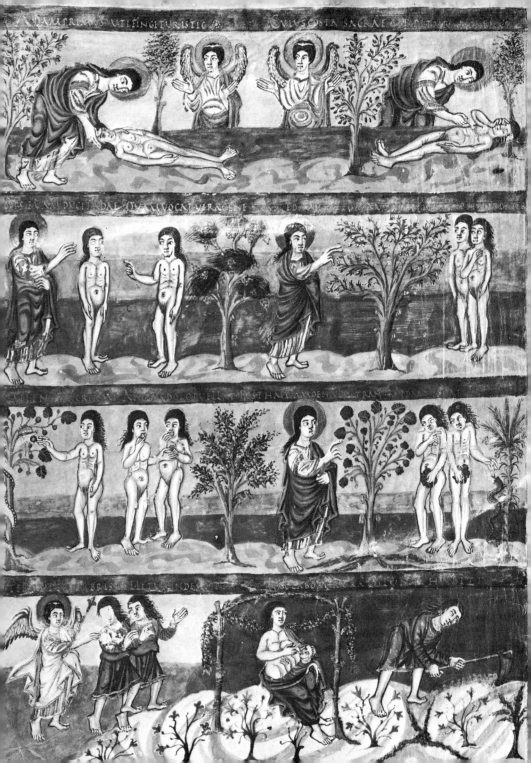

women in their houses. The bishops were to supervise the clergy and make sure that Mass was said, and baptisms performed regularly. The bishops were to hold regular visitations of their clergy, and self-styled wandering bishops and wandering priests were to be supervised. Lands which had been alienated were to be returned to the Church.

By these and similar measures, the administration of the Church was to be improved. The programme of reform found the firm support of Carlman, an uncle of Charlemagne's, and to a lesser extent of Pepin, Charlemagne's father. Both men were at that time still no more than the chief officers presiding over the households of the last Merovingian Kings. It struck them that a well-organised system of Church administration would contribute much towards strengthening their own authority over the far-flung regions of the kingdom. In order to consolidate unity, they even sought the support of the Pope in Rome. The Popes were at first rather reluctant to be drawn into the problems of the Frankish Church—for they were fully occupied with affairs in Rome. Only as it became increasingly clear to them that their own power in Rome was being threatened by the growth of the Lombard kingdom in Italy in the middle of the eighth century and only when they began to realise that the emperors of Byzantium were less and less in a position to offer help in Italy, did successive

Pope Leo, Charlemagne and St Peter. Mosaic of Lateran Triclinium Arch, Rome, as restored in the eighteenth century

Popes understand that it was in their own interests to co-operate with the growing power of the chief officers of the Merovingian Kings' household.

But in the Frankish kingdom there was to be very formidable opposition to such an outrageous programme of ecclesiastical reform. The magnates realised that a reform movement would deprive them not only of all the benefits they had reaped from the assimilation of bishops to their own class but also of the continuing alienation of Church lands. And as Pepin was preparing to usurp the Crown, he needed all the support he could get from the magnates. He,

Christ in Majesty from the cover of the Codex Aureus of St Emmeram

therefore, toned down the reform programme and became increasingly reluctant to push it forward.

When Charlemagne became King in 769 in succession to his father, he sized up the situation very realistically. On one side he understood that if he could maintain some kind of ecclesiastical discipline, he would be able to exercise power through the bishops as well as through the counts. On the other side, he realised that, if he pushed the ecclesiastical reform programme to its limits, he would antagonise the magnates on whose support he depended and whose community of interest provided the one uniform and coherent bond throughout his vast and heterogeneous dominions.

As a result he did nothing much to enforce a strictly clerical tenor of life among his bishops. On the contrary. He appointed bishops as it suited him and his magnates, and continued to disregard the canonical prescription that a bishop ought to be elected by his clergy and his flock. He admonished his bishops to exercise a certain restraint as far as women and drinking and hunting was concerned. But he did not follow such admonitions up. And, above all, he expected both bishops and abbots to render military service like all the other magnates and often enough he entrusted them with special military tasks. He considered them his very special officials and often granted them an immunity from royal power—which meant in practice that they were to exercise on their lands the power which ought, more properly, to have been exercised by the King's agent, the count. Thus the bishops were encouraged to live and function like royal officials and were charged with the administration of justice and the raising of troops.

In some cases Charlemagne appointed men of very lowly origin as bishops because he considered them specially suited for the task. Such appointments met with the criticism of the magnates, who felt that they were being deprived of their right to such appointments. But the men of lowly origin who became bishops were subject to a special temptation. In order to keep their end up, they often endeavoured to imitate the style of life of the local magnates to a grotesque degree in order to prove that they had arrived and were as good as the local magnate. Moreover, they followed the magnates' example of promoting the fortunes of the members of their family with a vengeance. Charlemagne showed very little inclination to

Einhard's church at Steinbach, Germany

promote rigid stan-
dards of clerical
behaviour and
stubbornly refused
to set up a hier-
archy of bishops:
he did not want to
create metropoli-
tan districts with
an archbishop at
the head, lest such
an archbishop take
it on himself to
enforce clerical
standards among
the bishops of the
archdiocese. When
he did eventually
give way to a
certain amount
of pressure and
appointed arch-
bishops, he did so
in a way which
would curtail the
authority of these
metropolitans, for
their spheres of

The ecclesiastical hierarchy from the Sacramentary of Marmoutiers

competence were not geographically defined, except in very rare cases.
And this meant that any bishop who wanted to subtract himself from the
supervisory authority of an archbishop could do so.

Charlemagne's policy therefore tended to have a double result. In so
far as the King appointed the bishops, insisted on some basic educational
attainments and issued precise instructions as to how they were to com-
port themselves, the tone in the Church was raised. But in so far as he
refused to set up metropolitan sees and was unable to forge devices for
enforcing his admonitions, he continued to countenance the monopoly

of the wealthy land-owning families to whom Church offices were, like secular offices, means of further enrichment. In this way, Charlemagne established some kind of balance: Church discipline improved enormously during his reign; but the bishops did not become a separate class of office-holders and landed proprietors, set apart from the magnates and the royal family. But the promotion of a few outstanding churchmen during his reign and the improvement in the tone of episcopal life laid the basis for the separation which in the two generations after his death was to upset the balance.

In the meantime, however, the tone was certainly raised. Bishop Leidrad of Lyon reported to the King that he had been able to train a clergy in his diocese by setting up a school, acquiring suitable garments for them, and buying a few of the objects necessary for proper church services. The services themselves were being performed according to the model of the liturgy practised in the royal chapel. From another bishop we know that he held regular visitations. He assembled priests and canons, monks and laymen in a church and addressed them in turn. He asked the priests whether they knew the Apostolic Symbol and the Lord's Prayer, the penitential rules and the basic law of the Church, and whether they knew how to say Mass, perform baptism and preach. He then turned to the monks and asked similar questions and finally even admonished the laity to see to it that their children grew up with the proper instruction.

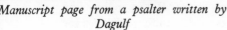

Manuscript page from a psalter written by Dagulf

Preaching a sermon from the Utrecht Psalter

Officially it was laid down that everybody should know the Lord's Prayer and the Catholic faith in the Holy Trinity. Godparents were supposed to teach it to their godchildren and those who did not know the prayer and the faith were not allowed to be godparents. According to some regulations priests were even required to know the Ten Commandments by heart and to teach them to their parishioners. According to others, every member of the congregation should know by heart the Creed and the Lord's Prayer and should even be able to join the singing of the *Sanctus* and the *Gloria Patri*. But one cannot possibly imagine that, in a society in which illiteracy was so universal and in which there were so few schools for the training and instruction of the clergy, regulations of this kind were anything but pious hopes. At best, the communal chanting of the appropriate formulas was a ritual; at worst—and this was true for the majority of cases—nothing much took place at all. Similarly, there was an order that bishops and priests were to deliver sermons. But preaching was at a very low ebb. When a priest was able to preach a sermon, it did not take the form of a moral exhortation. The Carolingian sermon, if one can speak of such a thing, was a fairly rudimentary attempt to cast 'the light of knowledge' on some key concepts of theology like grace and love. This kind of wisdom was not a religious, let alone a spiritual, exercise, but an educational declaration. It was a show-piece, a collector's item.

More important than preaching was the reading of homilies. Here again, there was an acute shortage. The authorities recommended a collection of homilies which had been specially compiled by Paul the Deacon. Paul had gone through a great many treatises and sermons of the Fathers and had collected a number of suitable passages from them in two volumes, enough for the whole ecclesiastical year. According to Alcuin, one of Charlemagne's scholarly friends, some bishops would not allow their clergy to preach and told them to confine themselves to the reading of homilies. Alcuin was indignant; but, given the low level of education of the clergy, one must suspect that the bishops meant well—for there was no saying what a priest might tell his congregation, whereas homilies were ready to hand and collections of homilies for such purposes were being prepared officially under royal instruction and in 813 an order was issued that they were to be translated into the peasants' patois, be it Romanic or *theodisk*.

It was not the least merit of Charlemagne's fatherly interest in ecclesiastical administration that he promoted a rigid uniformity in order to overcome local idiosyncracies and the garbling and debasement of doctrine and liturgy which necessarily resulted from an almost complete absence of education. He promoted uniformity not so much for its own sake but because he realised that there would be a general improvement if a set model were followed. He tried to obtain the set model from what seemed to him the oldest and most authoritative of traditions, Rome.

Charlemagne was no slavish follower of Rome. If anything, the city itself and the problems of its bishop were somewhat outside the limits of his political interests. For that matter, the Popes themselves did not exactly put themselves out to become involved with the Frankish Church. But it was in their interest to keep Charlemagne content, because they often needed his protection. They needed it against the

A page from the Gregorian Sacramentary, written at Cambrai

Canon Tables from the Book of Kells

Crucifixion

Lombards; and, after the defeat of the Lombards, against the factions in Rome. But it was not always easy to satisfy Charlemagne. On one occasion, for instance, he applied to Pope Hadrian I for a copy of the *Sacramentarium Gregorianum,* which was to serve as a model in Frankish churches. But Hadrian was not able to supply a copy of the original and sent a shortened copy of a later version. Charlemagne, fortunately, was no purist. He commissioned one of his scholars to make suitable additions and incorporated a great many passages from other sacramentaries current in Gaul. Many copies were made and, with a suitable preamble, widely distributed to Frankish churches. Even so it signally failed to establish a uniform standard for the celebration of the Mass.

On another occasion, when Charlemagne paid a courtesy visit to Rome in 774, Hadrian presented him with a copy of the collection of canons by Dionysius Exiguus prefaced by a dedication in unbelievably barbarous Latin verse admonishing him to follow these directions. Although this version of ecclesiastical law was made universally binding in 802, and although the original was kept in Charlemagne's library and he caused a great many copies, all bearing a certificate to the effect that they were true copies, to be distributed, little was done to make this collection officially binding upon his clergy. If Charlemagne had enforced these canons he would have been obliged to insist on the free elections of bishops and on standards of discipline which were intolerable to his magnates. Whatever guidance he sought from the Pope, he always made it quite clear that he never thought of the Pope as a source of authority. 'My job', he explained once, 'is to order and organise; your job', he said to the Pope, 'is to pray for the success of my plans.'

Charlemagne was not only no purist, but also little interested in tasks which were not immediately practical. As is to be expected, all the current texts of the Bible were grossly corrupt and showed wide divergences. Charlemagne did not consider the production of a standard text a matter of importance—it was left to the private initiative of some scholars. Theodulf, the Bishop of Orléans, attempted an edition with the main variant readings. Alcuin, less ambitious, produced after many years of toil a text freed of the grossest corruptions, which he eventually presented to Charlemagne either on the occasion of his coronation as emperor or on the first anniversary of the coronation. The text was kept in his monastery of St Martin's at Tours and there a large number of copies were made and distributed to other monasteries and bishops during the ninth century.

Charlemagne's attempts to reform the Church were not only tempered by his practical concerns and his sensitivity to the interests of the magnates on whose support and co-operation he depended. His very understanding of the Christian religion was limited by the rural environment in which he lived. He could not possibly have an intimation of the spiritual problems, the psychological incentives for asceticism, the role of charity in personal relations—all features of the religious life of urban communities. When his learned friend Alcuin propounded to him the merits of

A page from the Heliand

Stoic temperance and moderation and the cardinal virtues, it occurred to his royal disciple that there was apparently very little difference between the teaching of the ancient philosophers and the teachings of the Christian religion. Alcuin agreed and explained that the sole difference between the philosophy of good common sense and the Christian religion was in 'faith and baptism', i.e. in a belief in the truth of certain theological dogmas and in the performance of an initiation ritual. There were occasions when Alcuin's theological imagination carried him further. Alcuin was a keen believer in allegorical interpretations and was prepared to think up the most complicated allegorical explanations why the Sundays before Quadragesimal were named after the numbers 60, 70 and 80 even though these numbers did not correspond to the numbers of days in question. Charlemagne brushed all this aside and insisted on a plain answer and on cold reasoning.

Even the most central elements of Christianity were understood in a concrete manner and interpreted in terms of the fighting and feuding customs of the age. There was no mention of Jesus' advice about the 'lilies of the field' or his concern with the innocence of little children or the Sermon on the Mount. Nor was there any interest shown in the mystery of sacrifice and resurrection. The cross was the instrument through which the Devil had been vanquished: it was the flag under which the Christian army had defeated the lord of evil. Eternal life was the reward on which faithful soldiers could count. And people who refused to fight under the banner

A Carolingian church

would be excluded from Paradise. Religious piety was thus equated with a man's loyalty to his lord. And when, a few years after the final pacification of Saxony, a Saxon poet wrote a vernacular poem about the life of Christ, he represented Christ as a war-leader and his disciples as his noble-born warriors. The marriage at Cana is a Court feast and the Sermon on the Mount reads like a barbarian chief's address to his faithful followers. As is usually the case, Christianity had been able to contribute its share towards the destruction of the ancient tribal societies. But it could not, of itself, and as a mere body of doctrine, shape a new society and therefore, as people were regrouping themselves round the landed estate, religion was assimilated to the new social needs.

Imago hominis (*the image of man*). *The symbol of St Matthew in the so-called St Willibrord Evangelistary*

If Charlemagne imposed definite limits upon the reform of the episcopate and did not wish to encourage the bishops to disentangle themselves from the secular magnates, the lives and behaviour of the lower clergy were completely beyond his and the bishops' reach. There were a few priests who were attached to and officiated in independent churches, that is in churches built on free land. They were very exceptional—most of them had established themselves on land cleared by their own labour and were thus subject only to the local bishop. The vast majority of churches and chapels were built on land which was owned by a landed magnate. Any large landowner, especially when he was lucky enough to obtain a relic, might set aside a piece of his land, dedicate it to a saint and build a church or chapel on it. But he would continue to regard both the land and the church as his own private property and dispose of it according to his wishes. If he was generous or wished to acquire special merit, he might turn the land into a separate domain large enough to support tenants and serfs of its own, dependent on the church. But, in all cases, the establishment remained part of the original domain. Many such establishments were no more than additions to the lord's estate, like the stables or the mill. This practice seemed quite reasonable; and, at any rate, in an age when no other effective provision for the material support of the priest who was to officiate in the church could be made, this seemed a sensible economic arrangement.

As the church and its lands, however, remained the property of the magnate, he enjoyed the right to appoint the priest, and he thus enjoyed a complete control over the way in which that priest officiated and carried out his tasks. To begin with, it was quite often difficult to find a priest willing to be put in charge. It was almost impossible to get hold of a trained man. But even untrained people were not anxious to be turned into priests, even though the restrictions imposed on their way of life and the degree of asceticism expected of them were not substantial. Sometimes young men of landed families would choose the Church as a vocation, but in such cases their families and sometimes the King in person tried to dissuade them. On the whole, the temper of life provided little incentive for a freeman to vow never to bear arms again and not to participate in the *mallus*, the communal gathering in which 'justice' was dispensed. Unlike later centuries, there was no educational system and no learning which could entice those well-born young men who had no taste for the coarse pursuits of their brothers and cousins to seek a clerical career. As a result, a lord who needed a priest for his church had to choose one of his serfs who could not resist and have him ordained against his will by the local bishop—a magnate himself and perhaps the lord's brother or cousin and therefore ready to oblige. In some cases the village idiot or some other yokel was chosen because he was of no practical use to the manor. The lord also had a special incentive to make sure that the priest he chose would be compliant. It was one thing to acquire merit in the eyes of God by building a church, but nobody wanted to carry religion so far that it became an impediment to ordinary pursuits and lusty appetites. A priest was therefore expected to remain a servant in the proper sense of the term and not to molest his lord by demanding strict obedience to fasting or making irksome spiritual admonitions. The priest was expected to say Mass, but, for the rest, he was treated like a household servant. He was expected to wait at table or lead the hounds for the hunt and, if he was disobedient, he was flogged.

These conditions did not contribute to the prestige of the clergy. The higher positions, the bishoprics, were, with very few exceptions,

reserved for the members of the land-owning upper class. The lower positions were occupied by serfs or retainers. Naturally, a self-respecting freeman did not wish to enter the priesthood if it meant being treated like a household servant. Since it was impossible to recruit suitable people, the standards of behaviour left very much to be desired. In the generation before Charlemagne, there had been frequent complaints that the priests who administered the sacraments had never been baptised themselves—one shudders to think what the ritual performed by such priests was really like. Their behaviour was as coarse and rugged as that of the peasants from whom they

The four Evangelists

had been recruited. They wore no clerical garments and belched and spat during Mass, such as it was. They were given to heavy drinking and their way of life in no way differed from that of the local villagers. They would carouse with their neighbours and sleep away from home, they lived with women and, to supplement their meagre income, joined armed bands who robbed or fought others. Some men of very lowly origin showed a great deal of native wit and used the Church to advance their private fortunes. First, as serfs, they connived at being ordained—a practice which was as common as it was uncanonical. Then they used their standing as priests to fleece their parishioners and used the money intended for the upkeep of divine service to buy their own freedom. They then acquired land and serfs of their own. The complete lack of ecclesiastical supervision created any amount of opportunity for this kind of social mobility.

There were a few occasions when this intimate knowledge of popular customs derived from their own background resounded to the advantage of religion. When the Frisians, at the end of the eighth century, rose against Charlemagne, the missionary Liudger, whose own work among the Frisians was thus brought to a standstill, sent a bard who was well versed in their traditional songs and empowered him to perform emergency baptisms. But it was exceptional that such acquaintance with folk customs was used for the advance of religion. In most cases the priests remained an indistinguishable part of the society of their parishioners and lived by their customs. There were many priests who performed animal sacrifices, obviously in response to folk demands. Others performed rituals in connection with the winter solstice, acted as soothsayers and blessed amulets or performed sacrifices for the dead. One is not far wrong in seeing them more often as medicine-men and local sorcerers than as Christian priests.

Charlemagne tried to improve matters. Already, under his father, the tithe had been instituted in order to provide an orderly material subsistence for the clergy. Charlemagne tried to enforce its universal payment. But, in most cases, the tithe only led to further abuses which followed from the social system. The bishops sought to appropriate it and, instead of using it for the maintenance of their churches and the support of the clergy, they pocketed it themselves. The secular magnates sought to benefit from it by claiming that if it was paid to a church they owned, it was ultimately a rent due to them. Such priests as were dependent on it had to seek material support in other ways. They were eager to obtain an office on a magnate's domain in order to supplement their small income. They devoted more time to the pursuit of material advantages than to the performance of their ecclesiastical duties and 'many work night and day to acquire, through usury, worldly possessions, chattels, slaves, wine and grain'. Charlemagne was rightly indignant when such matters were reported to him. But, owing to the very nature of the social system on which his power depended, he could not take any steps to interfere.

Nevertheless, slight improvements were effected. The establishment of some episcopal schools helped with the elementary education of the clergy. There were now some priests who could read Latin and the greater diffusion of the accurate knowledge of the liturgy helped priests to carry out their ecclesiastical duties somewhat more punctiliously. The priests were not expected to live up to the standards required for bishops, but they were now expected to observe the fast-days, to commune regularly and not to accept gifts for the administration of the sacraments. Directives of this kind remained expressions of pious hopes. But they showed that, at least ideally, attempts were being made to detach the priests from the peasant background from which they had emerged and to which they belonged socially.

7 The Monks

One of the most direct and powerful effects of the spread of Christianity on ancient as well as medieval life was the propagation of the idea that a truly religious life was a life of withdrawal from society and from its economic, military and sexual obligations. It was based on the conviction that a truly religious life could never be a half-measure and that a mere participation in the sacramental life of the Church at certain set times while going about one's ordinary business in the intervals was, at best, a sorry compromise. Some people, therefore, decided to lead a truly religious life centred upon the pursuit of ascetic ideals of renunciation and fully devoted themselves to prayer. Instead of partaking of the sacraments at certain times, they made the whole of their lives into a sacrament. Some did it on their own, leading the lives of hermits; others combined into communities organised according to definite rules.

Monastic societies were established in southern Gaul long before the Frankish invasions. In some of these monasteries, especially at Lérins, situated on a small island opposite the modern city of Cannes, the monks followed the most sophisticated rules of asceticism framed to lead to great heights of spiritual contemplation. They had been introduced into Gaul in the fifth century at the monastery of Lérins by no less a person than the great Cassian himself, the most sophisticated psychologist and teacher of Neoplatonic metaphysics. Cassian's manuals of monastic psychology and discipline were held up as the ultimate goal even by St Benedict of Nursia, the founder of Western monasticism, who considered his own *Rule* only as a preparatory step for the final attainments of contemplation aimed at by Cassian. From Lérins the influence of these teachings had spread northwards as far as Verdun and Trier, where pupils of monks trained at Lérins had, from time to time, been bishops. But, as a result of the Frankish invasions, the high spiritual culture of these monasteries had suffered a rapid decline, and little remained of the attainments of Lérins after the establishment of the Frankish kingdom in the sixth century. This was only very partially due to the direct ravages of the invasions. The greatest damage was

The abbey of St Riquier. A seventeenth-century drawing after an ancient miniature

self-inflicted. From the sixth century onwards the Church and, with the Church, the monasteries, began to distrust education. This distrust was caused by a lack of sophistication. To the unsubtle Christian mind of the sixth and seventh centuries the conflict between Christian truth and irreligious falsehood appeared as a simple contrast between Christianity and ancient culture. As they rejected ancient culture, they rejected education as such because education was of necessity associated with Latin and with ancient, that is, pagan, authors. With the decline of education, there also set in a lack of understanding for the more sophisticated aspects of Christian theology and the worst sufferers were the monks and their spiritual aspirations. They lost touch with the subtle metaphysics and psychology of the Greek world on which men like John Cassian had based their spiritual guidance for monks.

If there was a rapid decline in the spiritual culture of the monks, there were nevertheless two factors in monasticism which assured the survival of the institution. The first factor was that a monastery was very adaptable to rural and agricultural conditions. All it needed was a plot of land which the monks could cultivate or which they could lease to tenants, servile or free, for the monastery to become a landed estate and to hold its own with any other domain or villa. The other factor lay in the nature of the case. A monastery was a religious institution. It was built round a holy place, its monks guarded and harboured a holy relic or the tomb of a saint. As such the monastery always became a place of worship and religious cult for the surrounding countryside. And, if the spiritual progress of its monks left almost everything to be desired, it tended to become a focus for the belief in miracles and the supernatural in general for the population of the district. People ceased to regard the monastery as a society set apart from the world and began instead to look upon the monks as the guardians of the holy and supernatural power enshrined in the relic.

It so happened that the magnates of the Frankish kingdom developed a very personal and special interest in these monastic foundations. Among the ancient Germanic tribes there had been many families who had stood out because of their special connection with a heroic or semi-divine ancestor. The disappearance of paganism had destroyed this foundation for pre-eminence. And now the magnates sought to support their landed wealth and the privileges it brought by a new charisma. Christianity offered an obvious opportunity in the worship of saints. As a result the early centuries of the Frankish kingdom in Gaul abound with saints—but almost without exception they are members of the wealthy and powerful families. In more ancient days, one of the essential marks

A reliquary

of sainthood had been poverty, lowly origin. A saint did not necessarily have to be born in a manger, but he had to have lived in one. Humility was the hall-mark of sainthood. The Frankish saints in Gaul were different. They belonged to the wealthy families. Although they had to strike certain ascetic attitudes sooner or later, they were all men and women who stood in life as warriors and landowners, as builders of splendid churches and impressive monasteries. Far from wearing the clothes of the poor and sharing the lives of the lower classes, the new saint was a man of 'aristocratic' bearing and usually his flight from the world took no

Flagellation. Utrecht Psalter

more extravagant a form than the transfer of a valuable relic to a newly founded monastery of which he might become the first abbot. In this way the land-owning classes established their right to pre-eminence by making it clear that certain members of their families had special religious merit and this merit helped to justify the wealth of the family.

As a result of these pressures and aspirations old monasteries grew rich by new donations, often scattered over a wide area; and new monasteries were founded throughout the kingdom and beyond. Economically they were large landed estates, the revenue of which was shared among a certain number of monks rather than monopolised by the family of the owner. But, just because so much wealth was involved, only certain people could be admitted as monks and the headship of the institution was in most cases reserved for the members of the family of the founder. All in all, such monasteries remained really part of the landed property of the founder's family. And while they did thus not essentially diminish his landed wealth, they very ostensibly contributed greatly to the charisma and religious renown of the family concerned. In this way, monasticism, far from being an alien or asocial institution, became an integral part of Frankish society.

The monks of these foundations lived according to a very wide variety of rules. In a very few cases, the Benedictine *Rule* was obeyed. In many more cases, the monasteries were organised according to the prescriptions of the Irish missionary, Columban. But for the most part the regulations of monastic life were an improvised mixture, and monastic discipline was not the strong point of any of these foundations. At the same time they performed a number of socially very useful functions. A monastery could function as a sort of prison for the confinement of high-born criminals, political conspirators, prisoners of war or hostages. Similarly, personal enemies could be forced to enter a monastery and a man involved in a blood-feud might be put beyond the reach of his enemies. This was, however, a double-edged sword. Many abbots were reluctant to receive as novices men who were involved in a blood-feud, because it had happened that their enemies had then regarded his new 'family', i.e. the other monks, as legitimate objects of their vengeance. In many cases abbots were more tough-minded and accepted unsuitable novices, without probation, against payment or a suitable donation which would enrich the institution. Obviously, the tone of life in monasteries accustomed to such and similar practices was not highly monastic. There was a great deal of drinking and high living and in many cases the general tone was much lower than that prevailing on an ordinary domain. For on the latter the owners all belonged to one family and their behaviour towards each other remained subject to the sanctions built into family life and clanship. But a monastery was usually a motley crowd of people whose loyalty to and consideration for each other was not subject to such personal restraints. Under these conditions it is difficult to decide whether the prevalent practice according to which the abbot was appointed by the actual 'owner' of the monastery, usually from among the members of his own family, was a blessing or a curse. If the monks had elected their abbots from among themselves or been allowed to offer the abbotship to a person they considered spiritually suitable, monastic life might have become even more undisciplined. But in most cases the monks knew where their interest lay. They knew that they needed protection from the magnates and that they would fare better under an abbot who had good family connections with them. Such an abbot, they reasoned, 'will defend us against counts and other mighty lords and his rank will incline even the Emperor's favour towards us. Do you know how he can do this? He can do it because he has rela- tives in the royal palace.'

Evangelist symbol and portrait from the Codex Millenarius

Charlemagne, as one might have expected, was no great friend of ascetic withdrawal, and it never occurred to him that the religious life ought to be promoted by the pursuit of ascetic ideals in monas- teries. His ancestors, like all the other magnates, had founded monasteries

in order to acquire religious merit in the eyes of God and charismatic power over their neighbours. But Charlemagne had arrived, and he therefore saw little point in devoting much wealth to further monastic foundations. He also issued orders to restrict recruitment for monasteries. Freemen were to enter a monastery only with special royal permission. Serfs were to be admitted only in small numbers and nobody, not even a serf, was to be forced to become a monk against his will.

But Charlemagne was a statesman, and, with a statesman's insight, he realised that monastic institutions, if properly regulated, could make an important contribution to the culture of his kingdom. With great acumen he recognised their cultural potential. He saw them as places of education and learning, and planned to utilise them as such into his administrative schemes. He was never troubled by the thought that, far from restoring monasticism to its original aims, he contributed further to deflecting monasteries from that aim by encouraging them to take up education and become centres of learning. He therefore decided to use his authority in order to promote the general acceptance of the most carefully and prudently drawn up of all monastic rules, the *Rule* of St Benedict. He sent to the monastery of St Benedict, Monte Cassino in Italy, for a copy of the genuine *Rule*, and had a great many copies of this made and sent to the abbots of many monasteries in his kingdom. He even had it translated into the vernaculer to make sure that monks ignorant of Latin would be able to profit from it. He ordered the *missi* to visit monasteries and he reiterated his injunctions for monastic discipline in countless letters and laws.

West end of St Peter, Fulda, Germany

In spite of the great importance which Charlemagne attributed to the *Rule* of St Benedict, in one important respect he did nothing to enforce it. According to the *Rule*, the monks were supposed to elect their own abbot. If this regulation had been enforced, the proprietary monastery would have come to an end. And, since Charlemagne's power was based on the support of the landed magnates, he could not possibly alienate them by encouraging a practice which would have deprived them of their monasteries. For that matter, Charlemagne himself 'owned' a large number of monasteries

St Germigny-des-Prés

to which he appointed the abbots, and he had no intention of curtailing his power in this respect. There are only four known instances in which he officially empowered monasteries to elect their own abbots—Lorsch, Fulda, Hersfeld and St Mary in Ansbach.

The monastic culture which Charlemagne helped to inaugurate and which flourished vigorously during the following century was, however, not solely based on the idea that a monastery, far from being a place of retreat set aside from the world, could become a centre of learning and education. The growth of monastic culture in the Carolingian age was also very intimately connected with the fact that a monastery was a landed estate—but an estate with a difference. The most important difference was that a monastic community, unlike the ordinary estate, consisted of a motley crowd of people. Given the very disorderliness of monastic life, there was frequently no telling whether the members of the community were monks, canons or neither. They were a crowd of individuals, each of uncertain status, who had come together, for holy or unholy reasons, and could be organised to run an estate on much more rational lines than an ordinary estate, because the status of the members of the community was flexible. The result was that it was much easier to introduce economic rationality in a monastery than in an ordinary estate where questions of status and rank, matters of duty and right, were rigid. The ninth-century monastery, therefore, developed economically towards greater prosperity and greater diversification of production and division of labour than most ordinary estates. In husbandry, horticulture, and the cultivation of special crops such as medicinal herbs the monasteries were soon far ahead of most ordinary estates.

The monasteries differed from other estates owned by magnates also in another respect. Thanks to the many pious donations due to the charisma to be derived from owning a monastery, many monasteries had become enormous estates. Alcuin, when he became Abbot of St Martin's in Tours, was said to be the lord of 20,000 human beings. The property of the abbey of St Germigny-des-Prés amounted to 221,187 hectares and contained 10,282 men. The monastery of St Wandrille owned, in 788, 4,000 manors and those of its 'canons' who owned only 200–300 *Hufen* were regarded as poor. Some held as many as 3,0co manors. The properties of a monastery were usually not contiguous. They were spread over a very wide area and stretched far into distant regions. In the year 900 we know of 434 settlements in Alsace, 399 of them containing lands owned by churches outside Alsace. The Abbot of St Martin's boasted that he could easily travel throughout the King's dominions without ever having to spend the night in a house other than his own. Some of the manors of the abbey of Fulda were 150 miles away from the monastery of Fulda and there was a distance of 40–50 miles between some of the manors of the abbey of Corbie.

These monasteries not only had large holdings; they also were spread over a vast area. Many abbots spent much of their time travelling from manor to manor to administer them. Only a fraction of the local produce was sent to the monastery. A large part of the production of each estate was used by the abbot and his entourage during his sojourn there and a further part was used for the upkeep of the monasteries own 'proprietary' churches in the region. The abbots of these monasteries therefore used part of their wealth to support parish priests. In this system, then, the influence and power of any one abbot was usually much more widespread and far-reaching than the influence of even

Mosaic, showing the Ark of the Covenant, in the apse of St Germigny-des-Prés

the wealthiest of the lay magnates.

The abbot of a large monastery was among the most powerful magnates of the kingdom. Hence the importance of a monastery being under royal or private ownership. The owner of the monastery appointed the abbot, and the complex of lands owned by the monastery and their far-flung influence represented a great deal of political power. When the ancestors of Charlemagne were on their way to the top, they not only tried to win the support of the landed magnates but also lured a great many Merovingian monasteries to their support. Not the least of the reasons for their ultimate accession to the throne was their success with monasteries. When the Anglo-Saxon missionaries spread in Gaul during the eighth century, a great many of their new foundations appeared on Carolingian lands and on the lands owned by the magnates who supported the Carolingians. And with the advance of the Anglo-Saxon missionaries, the influence of the Irish monks in Gaul tended to decline—a decline which contributed much to the loss of influence of the Merovingian family, because they had been the patrons of the Irish influence. We can see very clearly in the case of St Denys, near Paris, how monasteries were won over. On several occasions, in the middle of the eighth century, the ancestors of Charlemagne, then only mayors of the Merovingian Kings, decided questions of property in favour of the abbot of the monastery. When it became clear that the last Merovingian King was doomed, Abbot Fulrad finally decided to back the winning horse. He became one of the chief participants in the events which led to the fall of the Merovingians. His monastery threw its power and prestige behind the Carolingians, who soon established very special and personal connections with it. In 792, when the abbotship was vacant, Charlemagne gave the abbey to Fardulf, a Lombard who had betrayed the plot of Charlemagne's eldest son Pepin and who had to be rewarded for his loyalty. This Fardulf was a very special friend of Charlemagne and, by becoming Abbot of St Denys, he received the power and wealth which enabled him to give his friendship a great deal of material expression. Fardulf also built a special hall in St Denys to house the King. The hall was built 'after the old Frankish pattern', i.e. it was a Germanic wooden building and on another occasion he carried the precious relics of St Denys on a campaign to Saxony.

The ability to dispose of a monastery by the appointment of its

An Evangelist

abbot was, therefore, an essential element in the power structure of the kingdom. Charlemagne saw to it that his special friends became magnates by becoming bishops and abbots. In this way he was able to enlarge the circle of the original landed magnates who supported him. Bishop Angilram received the monasteries of Senones and St Trond, and Bishop Hildebald, the monasteries of St Cassius and St Florentine in Bonn. After the conquest of Bavaria, Angilram's power was further increased by the monastery of Chiemsee, Hildebald received the Bavarian house of Mondsee. These appointments were the safest method of planting trusted friends in a new region and of giving them the land which alone could assure their standing and influence there.

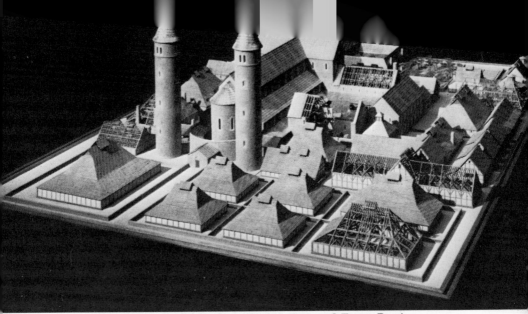

Model of St Gall monastery (Walter Horn and Ernest Born)

The monasteries of the age of Charlemagne, then, did not become great spiritual centres, but formed part of the rural economy of Frankish society. Some were even poorly endowed, so that the monks, such as they were, had to seek outside employment. Some were rich and allowed their monks to lead the lives of miniature magnates, as in the case of the old abbey of Fulda where land and grain stores had been divided among the monks so that everybody was free to go about his own business. And again in others the rapacity of a lay abbot had forced the monks to leave the institution and go about begging.

There were, however, some few monasteries which developed and flourished during the reign of Charlemagne and fully lived up to his expectation that a monastery should be a centre of civilised life and learning. Fulda, in spite of earlier decline; St Martin of Tours on the Loire; Reichenau on the island in the Lake of Constance, and St Germigny-des-Prés on the Seine and St Gall south of the Lake of Constance; Bobbio in Lombardy, and Lorsch near the east bank of the Rhine opposite Worms, were the most famous of these abbeys.

None of the original buildings of any of these places have survived. But the blueprint for the monastery of St Gall has come down to us and, with the help of excavations, historians have been able to construct a model of the abbey. The centre of the complex of buildings was the church, built as a basilica. It had a transept at the east end. There were apses at both ends and the west entrance was surrounded by a semicircular atrium. To the south of the church were the monastic buildings: the cloister, a dormitory, and, running parallel to the church, the refectory and the cellar. Beyond the church, at the east end, there were two more cloisters, one forming part of the novices' quarters and the other forming part of the infirmary. To the south of these buildings there was a cemetery and a vegetable garden. The monastic farm was situated in the west. There were stables for goats, sheep, pigs, horses and cows and a barn, a brew-house, a kiln and the kitchen. On the other side of the church, somewhat removed from the farm, there was the abbot's house, quarters for guests, the school and the *scriptorium* where monks were engaged in copying manuscripts.

It seems that the church and the buildings surrounding the cloisters were built of stone. Most of them were built like basilicas with a high central space lit by a clerestory. There was ample provision for fireplaces and the roofs were made either of lead or of thatch. The lesser buildings were made of wood and whitewashed plaster.

St Paul escaping from Damascus. Fresco from the south wall of St Procolo, Naturno, Italy

It is estimated that the sleeping accommodation and the storage space made provision for a community of approximately 110 and 140 servants and labourers. The whole monastery was self-contained. It had been St Benedict's intention in his *Rule* to make the monastic community independent of the outside world, and the ideal plan for St Gall was based on this prescription. Everything necessary for the life of the monks was to be found within the walls.

The well-run Carolingian monastery was an autarchic institution. As the influence of the Benedictine *Rule* was spreading and making itself felt, the monks' days were evenly divided between prayer and work. And, since the monks had no other problems to divert them, they were able to devote themselves rationally to husbandry, agriculture and horticulture, so that the estates run by monks tended to flourish economically. The monks attacked the wide areas of heath, waste and woodland which surrounded their monasteries and their dedicated labour attracted peasants who found that in the shadow of monastic walls they would find guidance for their own labour and eke out a better existence.

The well-run monastery produced a certain amount of surplus which was devoted to culture. Some monasteries established schools.

The four Evangelists writing their Gospels

But the most important contribution to culture made by these monasteries was the *scriptorium* and the library. In the *scriptorium* monks copied ancient manuscripts and illuminated them. The enormous collections of manuscripts copied in the monasteries of the ninth century are proof of their economic well-being, and the catalogues of these libraries afford some knowledge of the intellectual preoccupations of the monks. The monks who worked in the *scriptorium* had to maintain the strictest silence. In some of the manuscripts copied one comes across a couplet composed by the scribe bemoaning the cold weather or the hairiness of the vellum he had to write on. And some scribes might begin or end their copy of a manuscript by a personal statement with autobiographical details and the request that the reader pray for him. Since manuscripts were so rare and precious, a great many contained couplets invoking brimstone and hell-fire and eternal damnation for the man who might steal it, or an

Man killing a snake

exhortation to the reader to approach only with his hands washed and to hold the book carefully. The *scriptorium* was headed by the chief copyist, who decided what books were to be copied, who bought or borrowed them from other places and who assigned the work to the copyists. He also taught the art of writing to the younger copyists. The scribes sat on benches or stools and rested their feet on a footstool. They had no table but rested their work on their knees. The book from which they were copying was placed on a desk and their writing tools lay on a small table. There were quills from swans, geese and crows; a knife for sharpening the quills; and various kinds of ink in pots. They used compasses to measure the spaces between lines and a blunt long needle for drawing the lines.

By the eighth century, the ancient papyrus which had come from Egypt was no longer available. The monks, therefore, wrote on parchment made from sheep- or goatskins. The skins were first soaked in chalky water. Then they were stretched on a frame and scraped with pumice. They were then pressed and cut into sheets. Parchment had many advantages over *papyrus*. It resisted dampness and, if a text was no longer required, it could be scraped off and the same parchment could be used again. Even so, parchment was precious and we read of many an argument between the scribes and the administrators of the monastery who were stingy and refused to provide as much parchment as was demanded.

The sheets were handed to the scribes, who folded them together to make a copybook and each scribe might be assigned one part of the book for copying. In the end the sheets were collected. The head of the *scriptorium* would check them and have them bound into one volume covered with skin. As binding was laborious, many works were often bound into one volume.

One of the most remarkable, useful and lasting inventions of the Carolingian *scriptorium* was the development of a pleasing type of writing. It was a small letter, simple and elegant, which could be written and read with ease. It became known as the 'Carolingian minuscule' and was so loved by the Italian humanists of the fifteenth century that it was adopted by the printing presses. A great many of our present printing types are derived from it. This well-proportioned minuscule was its own recommendation. But the fact that it was used for the copies of Alcuin's famous Bible text, written in St Martin's of Tours, ensured its rapid spread.

Manuscript page

In Gaul the largest collection of books of the time was found in the monastery of St Martin of Tours. In Lorsch, east of the Rhine, the catalogue, though not complete, lists nearly 600 works. A very large proportion of these works were the writings of St Augustine and St Jerome. Profane literature was represented by Virgil, Lucan and Horace, by some of Cicero's speeches and letters, by essays by Seneca and Pliny the Elder. In the library of Fulda we find again that the works of St Augustine and St Jerome were given pride of place. But there were also parts of Tacitus, Suetonius' *Lives of the Caesars* and the *Letters* of Pliny the Younger. In St Gall the library contained the writings of such comparatively modern Doctors of the Church as Isidore of

Seville, Bede, Alcuin and Cassiodorus. There was also a sizeable collection of historical works by Eusebius, Josephus, Orosius, and a copy of the
very topical *History of the Franks* by Gregory of Tours. The library of
Reichenau contained treatises on grammar and some legal codes and
among the classical writers there was a copy of Ovid's *Art of Love* and of
Juvenal, of Plato's *Timaeus* and Sallust's *Catiline*. Perhaps the largest
collection of ancient authors was to be found in Bobbio in Lombardy.
The greater part of the library consisted of hagiography and theological
writings; but there were books by Terence, Virgil, Lucan, Juvenal,
Martial, Ovid and Lucretius.

It is worth stressing, however, that, if the monks were great collectors
and preservers, they were neither thinkers nor speculators. The age did
not produce a single book of criticism or of argument. Both ancient and
Christian authors were worshipped as monuments. It never occurred to
anybody to study and examine them and to investigate their relevance
to contemporary problems and knowledge. Even less did anybody worry
about the fact that these authors expressed very contradictory opinions
on all manner of things and that, if their writings were to be considered
as a body of truth, these contradictions ought to be discussed and ironed
out. In fact, such original writing as was done by people in the age of
Charlemagne shows almost no appreciation of the content of any of these
works.

There is only one indication of intellectual scruple. The earlier
suspicion of ancient pagan authors, which had contributed so much to
the rapid decline of ecclesiastical standards in Gaul, lingered on. In the
age of Charlemagne it had ceased to play a major part, but many people
were still troubled. When II years old, Alcuin, then a pupil at the
cathedral school of York, woke up one night and discovered a whole
crowd of hideous demons surrounding the bed of a slothful monk who
had not woken up in time for the Night Vigil. Alcuin was terrified by the
sight and vowed there and then that he would never 'hold Virgil dearer
than the Psalms of the Church'. It is significant that in Alcuin's lively
mind slothfulness was immediately associated with the enjoyment of
pagan authors and good literature. The old Christian trauma which had
contributed so much to the decay of learning and of the understanding
of Christianity continued to have its effects. Much later, Alcuin still
worried about the conflict and indulgently shook his head one day when

he watched one of his worldly friends: 'You ought to be fond of singing clerks; not of dancing bears!' As a mature man he did not keep his childish vow. But his experience was symptomatic of the widespread failure of his contemporaries, even of the most learned, to assimilate and personally appropriate the treasure of ancient knowledge which they so avidly collected.

8   The Scholars

In order to cement the bonds of society and to increase the feeling of association beyond the cold bonds which resulted from the community of interests of the upper classes, Charlemagne tried to promote a certain amount of basic education. He had a love of wisdom and learning for their own sake. There was much more than mere flattery in the verses which hailed Charlemagne not only as a zealous warrior but also as an indefatigable worker for the improvement of learning. His intentions, however, were always practical. He realised that the administrative system might be improved if a few people could be made to learn to read and write. He saw the necessity for elementary knowledge in arithmetic so that the moveable feasts could be determined with accuracy. He realised that the propagation of religious knowledge depended on an understanding of the Scriptures and on the clergy's ability to read the collections of homilies that were available.

He issued a great many instructions to bishops and abbots to establish schools near their cathedrals and in their monasteries. He criticised the illiteracy of the clergy and the uncouth language in which they expressed themselves. Some bishops and abbots

The Liberal Arts

followed his advice; many others probably neglected it. But, at his own Palace and in his own household, Charlemagne saw to it that instruction was provided.

Some kind of palace school in the ruler's household was a very ancient institution and it had never quite died out. Even the most primitive of his royal predecessors had issued some written documents and had to employ scribes to produce them. And these scribes had to be taught and trained in the royal household.

Under Charlemagne the Palace School was built up with great vigour. Charlemagne was fortunate in securing the services of Alcuin, an Anglo-Saxon scholar from York who became his lifelong friend. He had met Alcuin twice, once when Alcuin had been sent on a mission to Charlemagne, and again in 781, when he had run into him in Parma, Italy. Alcuin had acquired great renown as a scholar and teacher in York and, when he was about 50 years old in 782, Charlemagne persuaded him by generous promises and by holding out prospects of influential activity in his kingdom to join his household.

Alcuin brought with him a vast knowledge of classical and Christian learning, the traditions of which had always been more alive in the Anglo-Saxon kingdoms of Britain than on the Continent in Gaul. Under his tutorship the Palace School was completely transformed. It ceased to be a mere perfunctory introduction to primitive Court etiquette and became a genuine centre of learning.

The curriculum mapped out by Alcuin was very elementary. Ideally, the instruction was to be in the seven liberal arts, subdivided into the *trivium* and the *quadrivium*. The former included grammar, rhetoric and dialectic; the latter consisted of geometry, arithmetic, astronomy and music. Geometry was mainly concerned with a description of the earth, i.e. with what we would nowadays regard as geography, rather than with measurements. And there could be no advance in arithmetic at that time because the exclusive employment of roman numerals made any calculation other than the ones which could be done in the head impossible. In grammar, too, though the treatises of both Donatus and Priscian were known, great difficulties were experienced in understanding their precise definitions of the parts of speech, and there often remained a great gap between the memorising of the ancient grammarians' technical formulas and their practical application. Nevertheless, a great many manuscripts on all these subjects were copied and compiled in the eighth and ninth centuries.

At the Palace School the curriculum mapped out by Alcuin concentrated mainly on the study of grammar. Grammar was understood in a very wide sense 'as the science of letters and of right speech and writing; it depends on nature, reason, authority and custom'. Its subdivision included not only letters, syllables, words and parts of speech, but also the various forms of discourse, such as figures of speech, metre, stories and history.

In practice, instruction was mainly concerned with elementary knowledge. Alcuin spent a great deal of time teaching his pupils to distinguish the word *ara* (altar) from the word *hara* (pigsty) and to mind the difference between *acerbus* (bitter) and *acervus* (heap). He obviously had to pay greater attention to people who dropped their h's and to problems created by careless writing which confused 'b' with 'v', than to the more advanced problems of metre and story-telling.

St Matthew from the Coronation Gospels of the Holy Roman Empire

When he made use of Cicero, it was not so much in order to introduce his pupils to Roman history or Roman political thought, but in order to let them copy the correct form of address in letters.

As far as the substance of knowledge imparted in the school is concerned, it too consisted of very elementary pieces, a series of set answers to questions, phrased so as to act as a slight stimulus to the imagination:

What is writing?—The guardian of history.
What is speech?—The revealer of the spirit.
What gives birth to speech?—The tongue.
What is the tongue?—The lash of air.

What is the stomach?—The cook of food.

There were questions which not only stimulated the imagination but also imparted an elementary understanding of ethics.

What is man?—The slave of death, a passing wayfarer.
To what is man similar?—To an apple in the tree.
How is man placed?—Like a lantern in the wind.

And again, some questions served as an introduction to poetic metaphor:

What is the moon?—The eye of the night.
What is spring?—The painter of the earth.

Extract from the Third Decade of Livy, written under Alcuin's abbacy at Tour

There were also lessons in logical and mathematical thinking. The pupil was told that a ladder had 100 steps. On the first there sat one pigeon, on the second two, on the third three and so forth. How many pigeons were there on the ladder? The recommended method of calculation was somewhat cumbersome. The pupil was told to reflect that on the first step and the ninety-ninth step together, there were 100 pigeons; on the second step and the ninety-eighth step, again 100 pigeons and that only the fiftieth and the hundredth step had no pairs. The answer was therefore a simple sum: $49 \times 100 + 50 + 100 = 5,050$ pigeons.

On another occasion the pupils had to work out the answer to a problem which is still famous. There was a wolf, a goat and a cabbage. A ferryman was asked to convey all three safely across the river although his boat was able to carry only two of the three at a time. The wolf would eat the goat, and the goat the cabbage if left unattended. How could he carry out his task?

There is every reason to think that such elementary instruction was very beneficial to Charlemagne and the members of his household. But, whatever the benefit derived from formal instruction, the actual influence of Alcuin went beyond the curriculum of the Palace School.

Alcuin was not only a man who had, by the standards of the time, very considerable learning. He was a man who, partly through his innate gifts and partly through his literary culture, had highly developed sensibilities. His sensibilities ranged over a wide area. To begin with, he sported an unheroic attitude to life. He was neither a peasant nor a landowner—he was dedicated neither to labouring nor to fighting. And he wrote of himself when he joined the Court of Charlemagne, 'What business has the small hare among the boars, the lamb among the lions?'

For that matter, he was not an ascetic either. Though nurtured in a monastery, he was not a priest. He was, therefore, in every sense of the word, an outsider and belonged to none of the established orders of society and could rely on none of the sources of income on which the various orders could count. As a result he was somewhat anxious about his support and income. Charlemagne made lavish promises to him and he saw to it that they were kept. He enjoyed the abbacy of several monasteries and towards the end of his life, when he was too old and sick to travel with the Court, he became Abbot of St Martin of Tours, the wealthiest monastery in the kingdom, of which it was said that its abbot could travel from one corner of the Empire to the other without ever having to sleep in a house other than his own.

Since he was not an ascetic, he not only enjoyed the good food and drink at Court, but lent the weight of his classical learning to the justification of the pleasures of the table. He was not content with porridge and cheese but thought that beer and wine were necessary to promote good conversation. When he ate with the others, he took part in the conversation and raised its tone—he would quote some lines of poetry or produce a riddle to be solved and the conversation might turn on absent friends. One gains the impression that Alcuin introduced an air of culture into the lives of the rustic warriors who dominated the royal household.

On a deeper level, he introduced genuine poetry. He wrote much poetry himself in Latin and many of his verses are full of poignant feeling. He exploited nostalgia and friendship to the point of sentimentality in order to write very moving verse. His *Lament for the Cuckoo*, for instance, shows a deep attachment to a male companion who had left him:

O cuckoo that sang to us and art fled,
  Where'er thou wanderest, on whatever shore
Thou lingerest now, all men bewail thee dead,
  They say our cuckoo will return no more.
Ah, let him come again, he must not die,
  Let him return with the returning spring,
And waken all the songs he used to sing.
  But will he come again? I know not, I.

I fear the dark sea breaks above his head,
  Caught in the whirlpool, dead beneath the waves.
Sorrow for me, if that ill god of wine
  Hath drowned him deep where young things find their graves.
But if he lives yet, surely he will come,
  Back to the kindly nest, from the fierce crows.
Cuckoo, what took you from the nesting place?
  But will he come again? That no man knows.

If you love songs, cuckoo, then come again,
  Come again, come again, quick, pray you come.
Cuckoo, delay not, hasten thee home again,
  Daphnis who loveth thee longs for his own.
Now spring is here again, wake from thy sleeping,
  Alcuin the old man thinks long for thee.
Through the green meadows go the oxen grazing;
  Only the cuckoo is not. Where is he?

Wail for the cuckoo, every where bewail him,
  Joyous he left us: shall he grieving come?
Let him come grieving, if he will but come again,
  Yea, we shall weep with him, moan for his moan.
Unless a rock begat thee, thou wilt weep with us.
  How canst thou not, thyself remembering?
Shall not the father weep the son he lost him,
  Brother for brother still be sorrowing?

Once were we three, with but one heart among us.
Scarce are we two, now that the third is fled.
Fled is he, fled is he, but the grief remaineth;
Bitter the weeping, for so dear a head.
Send a song after him, send a song of sorrow,
Songs bring the cuckoo home, or so they tell.
Yet be thou happy, wheresoe'er thou wanderest.
Sometimes remember us. Love, fare you well.

In his *Strife between Winter and Spring* he introduced his listeners to the beauty of the seasons and his *Epitaph* for himself teaches a sensitive awareness of the transience of life and of the peace of death. He was obviously captive to classical sentiments when he wrote:

The world's delight I
followed with a heart
Unsatisfied: ashes am I,
and dust,

and Christianity enters into his thoughts no less conventionally:

Alcuin was my name: learning I loved.
O thou that readest this, pray for my soul.

There were poems in which he gave expression to his homosexual attachments and longed for the time when he could clasp his friend

with the fingers of desire . . . how
I would sink into your embraces . . .
how would I cover with tightly pressed
lips, not only your eyes, ears and mouth
but also your every finger and your toes. . . .

With these poems Alcuin heightened and refined the sensibilities of the Frankish Court and the royal household, and Charlemagne's devoted and lifelong friendship is proof that he met with some response. The following lament, written after his death by one of his pupils, is a moving example of such response:

O little house, O dear and sweet my dwelling,
O little house, for ever fare thee well!
The trees stand round thee with their sighing branches,
A little flowering wood for ever fair,
A field in flower where one can gather herbs
To cure the sick;
Small streams about thee, all their banks in flower,
and there the happy fisher spreads his nets.
And all thy cloisters smell of apple orchards,
And there are lilies white and small red roses,
And every bird sings in the early morning,
Praising the God who made him in his singing.
And once the Master's kind voice sounded in thee,
Reading the books of old philosophy,
And at set times the holy hymn ascended
From hearts and voices both alike at peace.
O little house, my song is broke with weeping,
And sorrow is upon me for your end.
Silent the poets' songs, stilled in a moment,
And thou art passed beneath a stranger's hand.
No more shall Angilbert or Alcuin come,
Or the boys sing their songs beneath thy roof.
Nothing remains in one immortal stay,
Bright day is darkened by the shadowy night,
Gay buds are stricken by the sudden cold.
A sadder wind vexes the quiet sea,
And golden youth that once would course the stag
Is stooped above his stick, a tired old man.
O flying world! That we, sick-hearted, love thee!
Still thou escapest, here, there, everywhere,
Slipping down from us. Fly then if thou wilt.
Our hearts are set in the strong love of God.

But the most important effect of Alcuin on the life of the Court circle was again a practical one. In order to raise the standard of public administration and rectitude, Charlemagne had sought to attract a number of young men to his Court to be educated there. He hoped in this way gradually to build up something like an Imperial staff of administrators. The formal teaching imparted at the school did not go very far. And often enough Charlemagne expressed his dissatisfaction because the young men, especially if they came from wealthy families, were bad scholars and proved lazy. It was not easy to break these young colts who came from rustic and uncouth backgrounds.

Alcuin's services in this direction were invaluable. His sensibilities and his feeling for friendship managed to pervade the whole Court and to introduce a personal and emotional air into the lives of these men. In this way he did much to weld them together into a group of friends, into a circle of people who were bound to each other by emotional attachments. And this was a very necessary and effective supplement to the formal education they received.

Alcuin cast his net wide. It was natural that the immediate members of Charlemagne's family should be drawn into the circle of friendship. Alcuin showed love and concern for Charlemagne's daughters and sons and made them aware of the feelings of friendship. He taught them to supplement the feeling of togetherness they enjoyed as

Part of a page of the earliest manuscript of Alcuin's letters

members of the royal clan by a personal note. He issued moral instruction, he listened to their emotional problems, but above all he introduced them to the beauty and tender gentleness of personal relations.

Next he sought to draw the household officials into the circle. The royal seneschal was one of his favourites. With much humour Alcuin wrote of his activities in the bakehouse and the kitchen. He made these men feel that they were loved as persons by the whole Court and were not just men whose duties and relations with other people were defined by their status. And in the same way he showered his feeling of fellowship on the chamber-

Canon Tables

lain and the cellarer. No doubt Alcuin was not wholly disinterested. If these people were his friends, they would look after his needs more willingly. But what really matters is that Alcuin taught gentle manners and courtesy based on personal relations.

Last, but not least, he established a sense of friendship and communion among the men who administered offices and estates, bishoprics and monasteries. The circle of friends headed by Alcuin contained only a very small fraction of all the many officials and administrators of the kingdom. But even so it was of the utmost importance that such a circle should have existed at all. These men kept in constant touch with Alcuin. They visited each other, wrote letters to each other and exchanged presents. In this way Alcuin cemented the official bonds of loyalty and duty by personal emotion and helped Charlemagne to build up a staff of reliable administrators.

There was Arno, who became the first Archbishop of Salzburg and who, as Abbot of St Amand, had been Alcuin's neighbour. There was Willehad, a young kinsman of Alcuin. He had worked as a missionary among the Frisians and later found refuge in the abbey of Echternach, headed by another friend of Alcuin, and in 787 he became the first Bishop of Bremen. Riculf succeeded Lul as Archbishop of Mainz. Alcuin wrote to him: 'How miserable it is that the people one loves are nearly always absent.' And Riculf, another time, made Alcuin a present of a comb and Alcuin thanked him as many times 'as my present has teeth'. Ricbod, the Abbot of Lorsch and Archbishop of Trier, was a special friend of Alcuin. He had been a student of Alcuin's and there were many complaints about his prolonged absence and his failure to keep up a regular correspondence. 'What has your father done, that his son should forget him?' Beornred was, like Alcuin, an Anglo-Saxon. He was Abbot of Echternach and later also became Bishop of Sens. Alcuin loved to stay with him at Echternach and, even though Beornred was employed on many diplomatic missions, he

St Mark writing underneath his symbol, the lion

found time to copy for himself Alcuin's commentary on the Gospel of St John. Alcuin exchanged gifts and warm letters with Remedius, the Bishop of Chur, and poems with Fardulf, the Abbot of St Denys near Paris. He wrote letters to Angilbert to exchange greetings and asked for relics from his monastery of St Riquier in western France. He wrote a verse inscription in honour of the erection of an oratory by Magulf, the Abbot of Fleury on the Loire and, when Itherius, the Abbot of St Martin of Tours (whom Alcuin was to succeed in 796), lay dying he wrote to him: '. . . I shall have no friends like you hereafter at St Martin's. We have served the world well enough these many days. Let us live unto God in the few that remain.

Maiestas Domini, Gundohinus' Evangelistary

Now read this with joy, begin with decision, fulfil in blessedness, and God be with you forever.' Like most other abbots of the time, Itherius had served as a royal envoy and administrator. Adalhard, the Abbot of Corbie and his brother, Wala, were cousins of Charlemagne. They became very special friends of Alcuin. Adalhard had quarrelled with Charlemagne over the attack on the Lombard kingdom. But Charlemagne forgave Adalhard and Alcuin helped to draw him into the circle of his friends: 'Please do not mind writing, because I so love to read your letters. It only costs you a little and it gives me so much joy.' And a young man from a wealthy family in Septimania by the name of Witza was taught by Alcuin at the Palace School, became his lifelong friend and later the leader of the monastic reform movement which was to flourish under Charlemagne's son and successor.

There is no point in giving a full list of all the members of the circle.

Christ and the four Evangelists

It contained not only men whom Alcuin had first met at the royal Court, but also a large number of men who had been his friends in Northumbria. His personal knowledge of their honesty and devotion was a great recommendation to them when they came to Gaul, to serve as missionaries and bishops and abbots. They served in Italy, in Saxony, in Britain and in every corner of Gaul. All these men rendered invaluable service to the King by keeping the far-flung Empire together. They were reliable and could be trusted, because they were all personal friends. Their standards of behaviour and relations with other people were not governed by clanship loyalties, feelings of tribal cohesion or, worst of all, by the personal greed which kept so many families together, but by their personal relationships, suffused with the gentle friendliness of Alcuin's admonitions.

One might almost conclude that Alcuin managed to turn the feeling of fellowship among these men into an institution. Apart from keeping up a constant correspondence, he also exchanged presents with them. Often enough these presents consisted of relics—and the demand for relics as a substitute for genuine spiritual elevation was very great. But, besides their religious significance, the exchange of such presents consolidated social bonds. And Alcuin's fellowship of administrators found that they were being held together not only by the emotion of friendship but also by an almost ritual habit of exchanging gifts. Furthermore, Alcuin introduced the custom of bestowing classical names on all his friends. There was a Homer, a Naso, an Antony, a Virgil, a Macharius, a Damoetas. Arno was known as Aquila (the Eagle) and Alcuin himself as Flaccus. Thus these men stood apart by their classical names—a fellowship of educated and honest men—from the rest of the population.

The moral advice imparted by Alcuin on request was not informed by great standards of spirituality or ascetism. Both these goals were alien to Alcuin himself and he could not attribute much importance to them in the atmosphere in which he was living. If Alcuin was worshipped as a saint after his death, it was not because of the spiritual heights he had reached or because of the contemplative

The Fountain of Life, from Godescalc's Evangelistary

life he had led. He admonished his pupils and friends to be honest, and to respect the bonds of friendship. He advised them not to seek fame and wealth and not to indulge overmuch in sensuous pleasures. He trusted that a little knowledge of classical moralists would confirm this advice and for the rest hoped that a progress of wisdom and a knowledge of ancient authorities would act as a sanction and a restraint. 'Advise everybody', he wrote, 'to obey the will of God; advise the King gently, the bishops with dignity and the princes with confidence.' If one considered such advice out of context, it would amount to no more than pious words. But, placed into the context in which Alcuin hoped it would operate, it was merely an intellectual or ideal superstructure over the fellowship he had created by personal friendship and which he was cementing ritually by the exchange of letters and gifts.

Te Igitur, *beginning the Canon of the Mass from Drogo's Sacramentary, Metz*

Alcuin also made a more theoretical contribution towards giving some of his contemporaries a hopeful outlook on society and history. He held that the ancient Roman Empire was truly a thing of the past and that it had been replaced by the Christian Church. For this reason it was believed that the Byzantine Emperors could have no special claim to represent divine authority on earth. On the contrary, since Christian orthodoxy was best upheld in the kingdom of the Franks, the ruler of that kingdom was the ruler of Christianity. And the Church was growing as Charlemagne extended the boundaries of his kingdom further and further by conquest. In this way Alcuin helped to forge a whole new philosophy of history in which the progress of the Church was identified with the growth of Charlemagne's power.

Towards the end of his life, Alcuin became more preoccupied with other-worldly things. He became conscious of the sins he had committed and of the dirt of the world in which he had wallowed. He began to fear the Last Judgment. 'We are all', he wrote, '*homunculi*, at the end of time.' He even wrote to the Pope and asked him to pray that he, Alcuin, might be forgiven his sins.

Whatever Alcuin's personal reasons for turning his thoughts towards the more spiritual implications of religion, he was clearly at the end of his life breathing the new air of piety which was to become more widespread during the reign of Charlemagne's successor. In the age of Charlemagne itself, such spiritual and pious considerations were for the most part quite unfashionable.

In the meantime, the finest monument to Alcuin's philosophy of history was about to be erected by Einhard. Einhard had first come to the Court as so many other young men had done, in order to be taught and to be initiated into the circle of Alcuin's friends. He had remarkable literary talents and soon acquired a very special reputation in the palace. He was short, and was given the affectionate nickname Nardulus, little Einhard. But Einhard was not only a good writer. He acquired an intimate knowledge of the royal household, he knew everybody and everybody's habits. According to a later legend he even became the lover of one of Charlemagne's daughters. Although the legend is almost certainly false, it has the air of fitting the circumstance. After Charlemagne's death he used his good knowledge of the public and private life of the King in order to compose one of the most magnificent biographical essays of medieval literature, the *Vita Caroli Magni*.

He not only gave a reliable account of all the outward events of Charlemagne's reign, but described the daily life at the Court and sketched a fine portrait of Charlemagne himself—his firmness, his generosity, his friendship for the scholars and his love of his family. Einhard took as his guide the ancient Roman writer Suetonius, who had specialised in the writing of the lives of ancient Roman rulers, and often enough he lifted whole phrases from his preceptor. But his plagiarisation was always judicious, and there is no strong reason for distrusting his account. And when the modern reader is too suspicious and wonders whether it was really possible, given the rude and primitive conditions of the age, for Charlemagne to have been quite so magnificent as Einhard said, he ought to bear in mind that up to a point Einhard's biography was a sort of image of the ideal ruler (that is, ideal for the prevailing conditions) which produced its own verification. For Charlemagne, like so many other members of the Court circle, was becoming acquainted with moral standards and public purposes derived from classical and Christian models. And they must have tried from time to time to live up to these ideals and to rise above the crude preoccupations and appetites which were endemic in the rural society in which they lived. We may therefore think of Einhard's picture of Charlemagne as an ideal picture; and yet regard it as evidence of the goals which Charlemagne and many of his friends tried to promote and to which they aspired.

9 Doctrine

The rapid and very advanced dissolution of tribal bonds in all but a few marginal regions of Charlemagne's dominions had led to a great deal of social mobility. All sorts of people were found on the roads, moving from palace to palace, from monastery to monastery. They eked out a living by entertaining the people who offered them hospitality. Some were living on their wits, others were criminals. Some pretended to be holy men and others were genuinely religious. Some worked miracles and others sold relics. Some pretended to be pilgrims to a holy shrine and others peddled goods. There were runaway serfs, servants who had decided to leave their masters. Some had been driven away from homes and families by famine, some went in search of fortune. There were a few bishops and counts who were wealthy enough to be able to purchase the goods offered by pedlars, and the pedlars would then set up more or less permanent stalls on the outskirts of the bishop's or count's palace.

Regular trade, however, was exceptional. For the most part these wayfaring people had few opportunities to enrich themselves or to contribute to the enrichment or comfort of other people. Even wealthy landowners had little cash to buy goods; and there were no workshops in which goods were being manufactured for sale. On the whole, this wayfaring population was therefore much more of a threat to security and order than a potential source of wealth. In an era when the whole of the economy is a subsistence economy and when every estate and manor is self-supporting and when there is very little division of labour, social mobility is not an advantage. In such an era only its disadvantages are obvious. It encourages criminality because the people who are on the move are not restrained by the sanctions built into family life and local attachments. Apart from this horizontal mobility, there was also much opportunity for vertical mobility. Enterprising individuals could blackmail or browbeat others into dependence or into genuine servitude. Office-holders, lay or clerical, could deprive freemen of their land and members of their family could use their connections in order to improve their standing. The 'magnitude' of any magnate could be increased by cunning or

Detail from the Altar of Volvinio, St Ambrose, Milan

aggression and if there was enough cunning and aggressiveness, many a man could become a magnate. If horizontal mobility merely led to disorder and to petty crime, vertical mobility was more tempting and more dangerous—for, although the weaker men could hardly resist being pushed down the ladder, a collision was always likely to occur between two upward-moving magnates who wanted to progress at the expense of one and the same man.

Charlemagne, therefore, was anxious to reduce social mobility to a minimum. Genuine travellers and pilgrims and diplomats from foreign rulers were under the King's protection. But all other wayfaring people were classed as outlaws and were considered dishonest. Jugglers and minstrels, beggars and harlots, cripples and highwaymen were all lumped together as undesirable rabble. Royal displeasure was by no means reserved for vagrants on the lowest rung of the social ladder. Irish wandering bishops, who had been very common in Gaul during the century preceding the reign of Charlemagne, were frowned upon. They were ordered to find a stable abode and to organise themselves into communities. On one occasion seven such bishops were assembled in the Upper Rhineland into a monastic community and settled on the land. There were people who wore a tonsure or a monastic habit but who were neither priests subject to a bishop nor regular monks. They were told not to drift about lest they 'confuse spiritual with secular business'. The existence of the many monasteries was a never-ending invitation to social mobility. For all sorts of reasons people could leave their families and their land and seek refuge in a monastery. Sometimes they wanted to avoid the consequences of a blood-feud they had caused, sometimes they entered a monastery for economic gain, and sometimes people were forced to enter a monastery which was short of monks. There was legislation against such indiscriminate flight into monasticism—not so much because the King was opposed to the growth of monasticism but because he did not wish to countenance the social mobility which such growth encouraged. Freemen were to enter a monastery only with royal permission—a rule which it must have been quite impossible to enforce. Serfs were not to be sent into a monastery against their will. Last but not least, Charlemagne encouraged the growth of feudal bonds. He estimated that it was better for a poor man to become a wealthy man's vassal than to cherish his own freedom and independence.

On all fronts he encouraged and promoted the trend towards hierarchy and social stability. Given the fact that the economy was rural and closed and geared to mere subsistence, no good purpose could have been served by social mobility. At best it led to insecurity; at worst to crime. It could never lead to a division of labour and a corresponding rise of the standard of living. But here Charlemagne faced a dilemma. He disapproved of the injustice caused by the advance of certain people and feared the disorder occasioned by competition in the upward move among the magnates. But in so far as he encouraged his magnates to enrich themselves at other people's expense, so that society could be ordered hierarchically and become more stable, he had to condone the very evil which he wanted to combat. In order to achieve a certain measure of integration over so vast an area, people had to be ordered hierarchically—the top layer in direct touch with the King and every other layer linked to the King indirectly. It would have been completely impractical to aim at a direct demonstration of loyalty from every single inhabitant of the King's dominions. But in order to promote hierarchy, Charlemagne had not only to tolerate but actually to encourage vertical mobility, so that the forces making for integration were at the same time the forces

St Luke

which disturbed it most.

In order to promote unity, stability and hierarchy and to make up for the ambivalence of vertical mobility, Charlemagne and his scholar friends threw their whole weight behind the propagation of the Christian religion. The teachings and the practices of Christianity are especially suited to promote sociability and cohesion of diverse peoples over a very wide geographical area. The doctrine that one must forgive trespasses and

St Mark

love one's neighbour regardless of his status, class, clan or family must not only have a strong levelling effect in any one group but must also lead to the cohesion of a large number of diverse people who, if they continued to be guided by their tribal or family or national interests, would find little in common.

Unfortunately, it was not possible for either Charlemagne or his scholar friends to understand Christianity in this sense, in which it would have been extremely useful. They were children of their age and were all more or less deeply caught in much more primitive religious conceptions. They all thought that the Christian religion they were so earnestly preaching and promoting was basically a tribal religion and that its chief merit was to define the membership and the limits of the tribe which had espoused it. The tribe thus envisaged was, of course, a very large one. Its members comprised very different kinds of people and its lands stretched from the Mediterranean to the Channel, from the Atlantic to the Elbe. But a tribe it nevertheless was. It was referred to as *populus Christianus*, the Christian people. The doctrines upheld by the tribe had nothing much to do with the love of one's neighbour or the forgiveness of sins or the brotherhood of all men. The bonds of religion were not provided by faith, hope and charity, but by the ritual of baptism and, for a small class of educated people, by dogma.

We have already seen how deeply Charlemagne himself was committed to pagan and tribal customs in his private family life. He only paid lip-service, if that, to the idea of Christian monogamous marriage. And, if this was the ruler's practice, how much more deeply ingrained must these customs have been among the people below him who had no obligation to please a few progressive clergymen and to make a public protestation of their Christianity. If we take another close look at Einhard's biography of Charlemagne we will also make a curious and telling discovery. For the main body of the work, Einhard modelled his description of his hero on what he had learnt from Suetonius to be suitable to a great ruler. When he reached the end and had to describe Charlemagne's death, we come across a very striking and significant deviation. Suetonius tells us that the Emperor Augustus died like a Stoic hero: Augustus told his friends that he had played 'the game of life' well, turned to the wall and died. Instead of reproducing a death-bed scene of this kind, Einhard, for once sensitive to the emotional atmosphere of the age of Charlemagne, devotes the chapter to a description of the portentous omens presaging the hero's death and then underlines the meaning of Charlemagne's death by describing how the whole vital force of the world seemed to be running down. He clearly wanted his readers to understand that Charlemagne was not just a civil magistrate but the living embodiment of the divine or magic power which sustained the universe; and that, with his physical decline and death, that power was running out. Einhard here, instead of deviating from his classical and Stoic model into Christian piety, deviates into the world of Stone Age paganism. When it came to the last things, Einhard abandoned all pretence of classical education as well as of Christian idealism and introduces his readers to the authentic air of the age. There was nothing there about the resurrection of the body and the hope of life everlasting. By comparison, the chapters which contain the description of Charlemagne's Christian burial and the Christian conventional formula which stood at the head of his last will and testament are nothing more than an outward formality.

And so it was that the Christian teaching was officially propagated and upheld in order to define the limits of the Christian tribe. Above all, it was necessary to see to it that the newly conquered pagan peoples were converted. They all had to undergo the ritual of baptism and, if they refused or renounced the newly acquired faith afterwards, they were to be punished by fire and sword. The penalty for burning a Christian church, for stealing its contents, for eating meat in Lent, for killing clergy or for celebrating a pagan rite was death.

Christ blessing—from the Evangelistary of Godescalc

The voice of Alcuin was sometimes heard pleading for a more spiritual approach to conversion. Alcuin warned that, if the heathen started associating Christianity with brutality, they would never make good Christians. He begged bishops to preach righteousness rather than to exact tithes and to nourish the new spirit of Christianity with the milk of apostolic kindness and not to place a harsh yoke on new converts. He even wanted baptism to be preceded by a confession of faith.

Alcuin's voice was crying in a wilderness. The most disturbing aspect of his failure to be heeded is the fact that he was actually proved wrong. Such as it was, Christianity taught by fire and sword made rapid progress among the Saxons once the backbone of tribal resistance was broken for good. And within a few decades of their final brutal conversion, a Saxon

The Fountain of Life from the Gospels of St Médard of Soissons

poet produced the first genuinely autochthonous piece of Christian literature, a long poem about the life of Jesus entitled *The Saviour*. It shows that the Saxon Christians understood the new religion in terms of their old tribal customs: Jesus was the lord who managed to become Matthew's master because He promised more generous rewards than the king whose 'thane' Matthew had been. Alcuin's fears had clearly been unfounded, for not even he could have hoped for anything better.

The uniformity and purity of the faith which kept the vast tribe together was, however, threatened not only by the newly conquered pagans. When the Spanish March was conquered from the Moors, an entirely new problem arose. Most of the inhabitants of the Spanish March, on both sides of the Pyrenees, were the Christian descendants of the Visigoths who had settled there during the fifth century. Their liberation from the Muslim yoke was a great relief to them; but it brought a great danger to the faith.

The Visigoths had espoused the Arian doctrine (officially condemned in 325 at the Council of Nicea) that Jesus, the Son of God, was neither as eternal as God nor consubstantial with Him, and that He was, albeit a Person of the Trinity, clearly a lesser Person than God Himself. In this crude form Arianism had disappeared even from the Visigothic churches in Spain. But it had given rise to the belief, very popular in the Church of Toledo, that Jesus had been a human being and that He had become divine and the Son of God by adoption. This belief, called Adoptianism, was an off-shoot of the old Arian doctrine and, when the Spanish Christians were liberated, they not only continued to uphold it themselves but began to spread it in Gaul.

Adoptianism was a great worry to Charlemagne and his scholarly friends because they proudly upheld the Nicene Creed and the belief that the three Persons of the Trinity were consubstantial, that Christ was fully divine just as He was fully human. For them Adoptianism was a heresy which, if allowed to spread, would not only destroy the purity of the faith but divide the tribe, the *populus Christianus*. Hence Adoptianism was officially condemned and proscribed and its chief propagator, Bishop Felix of Urgel, was eventually imprisoned in a monastery.

There was another occasion for Charlemagne and his theologians to do battle for the dogma of the Trinity. In the Greek Church at that time the practice had grown up of saying that the Holy Spirit had proceeded from the Father through the Son. This formula, however, reeked of heresy to the Frankish theologians because, if interpreted literally, it seemed to imply that the Holy Spirit had come from the Father and had emerged through the Son, i.e. that the Son's role was somewhat subordinate

Reliquary of Andenne

to that of the Father. The Frankish theologians suspected here a sort of Adoptianism in disguise; and, behind Adoptianism, a variant of Arianism. They entered the fray on behalf of the full equality of the Son with the Father and Charlemagne decreed that the correct formula to be used, in Latin, was 'from the Father *and* the Son'.

Towards the end of the eighth century, the question was not considered a matter of vital importance. Pope Hadrian was greatly perturbed when he learned of the vehemence with which the Franks insisted on their formula. To people less preoccupied with tribal uniformity than Charlemagne was it seemed a point of very minor importance, and the Pope would have much preferred to let everybody please themselves as to which of the two formulas they used. But Charlemagne was intransigent and the Pope had to go along with him. Frankish intransigence could, of course, not be extended to the Greek Empire and thus there emerged a major liturgical split between the Western and the Eastern Churches.

Charlemagne and his theologians were not only concerned to preserve the uniformity and purity of dogma which bound the *populus Christianus* into one solid tribe. They were equally anxious to work out a principle which would set their Christian tribe apart from all other Christians. This was no easy thing to do. The Christian religion was the only body of belief available at the time, and it was a misfortune that there were so many Christians outside the confines of Charlemagne's dominions. As a result it was found necessary, by hook or by crook, to define Christianity in a way which would include all the people living in Charlemagne's dominions and exclude all those who did not.

The opportunity arrived when the question of the worship of icons was raised. True to its Semitic origins, Christianity had at first shown the greatest hesitation in making and using pictures of God, of Jesus and of the events in the Bible. This was natural enough, because the refusal to make graven images set monotheism apart from all forms of paganism. But eventually, as Christianity spread outside the land inhabited by Semites, the Semitic tradition had to give way and it became very common for Christians to draw, paint and sculpt images of Jesus and symbols of God. Purists might have had their doubts all along, but whatever was thus lost in purity was gained for the propagation of the faith: in ages in which most people were illiterate the pictorial

Psalter illustration

representation of the events of the Bible was an indispensable method of instruction.

But in the Eastern Church, where the Semitic elements of Christianity remained comparatively strong, pictorial representations continued to be frowned upon. And in the middle of the eighth century, just prior to the reign of Charlemagne, there emerged a powerful movement in Byzantium which was determined to reverse the dominant trend. It decreed the destruction of all icons and supported the decision by the very respectable monotheistic argument that pictures ought not to be worshipped. Among the lower classes and the uneducated, as one might expect, a religious picture was always an image tempting to worship.

The wave of iconoclasm swept over the Byzantine Empire and was only halted by a measure of compromise at the Council of Nicea in 787. At that council a very sensible measure was agreed upon. A distinction was drawn between the respectful admiration of pictures and the worship of pictures. It was clearly laid down that religious pictures should

Opening passage of Libri Carolini

be used for instruction and as an aid to the imagination, provided they were looked upon with respectful admiration and not worshipped.

Iconoclasm, although it had reached those parts of Italy where Byzantine influence was still strong, had never become an issue in Gaul. Artistic production was, in the eighth century, in its infancy, and the whole question therefore seemed rather remote. But when Charlemagne and his scholarly friends were informed of the decisions of the Council of Nicea, they eagerly seized the opportunity of putting forward a definition of Christian orthodoxy which would exclude the Christians of the Byzantine Empire from the Christian tribe.

Fortune—or ought we to say misfortune?—played into their hands. The Latin translation of the Nicean decision which was delivered to Charlemagne was an unsophisticated and artless piece of writing which completely confused the all-important issue. It did not make it clear that at Nicea a careful distinction had been made between 'respectful admiration' and 'worship'. When confronted with this document, Frankish wrath knew no bounds. Everybody concerned jumped to the conclusion that it was clear proof that the Byzantine rulers were encouraging the worship of graven images and were little better than the children of Israel who had danced round the golden calf while Moses was absent on Mount Sinai. And since Charlemagne considered himself a David and a Moses in one, he unleashed a furious propaganda campaign against Byzantium.

Eventually somebody very close to the circle of Charlemagne's Court produced a major treatise, the so-called *Libri Carolini*, in order to attack the heretical practices of the Byzantine Empire and vindicate the Carolingian monopoly of orthodoxy. The treatise explained that God alone is worthy of worship and that pictures must on no account be worshipped. It then went on to explain that pictures were nevertheless valuable as aids to instruction and faith. The Byzantine decrees and indeed the whole Byzantine establishment were condemned, vehemently if unsubtly, as a 'moribund, degenerate megalomania'. In this way, the boundaries of the Christian tribe were defined: they coincided with the boundaries of Charlemagne's dominions.

The whole controversy was absurd. The doctrine about pictures put forward in the *Libri Carolini* is almost identical with the doctrine upheld by the Council of Nicea. But Charlemagne and his theologians were not aware of this. They had been misinformed. And since they were anxious to find a concept in terms of which to define the Christian tribe over which they ruled, they were not interested in setting inquiries afoot. They wanted to use the issue in order to parade as the chosen people who upheld the truth. When Charlemagne was described as the 'apex of Europe' this did not mean that he was the father of the West, as so many later historians have believed; it meant that he was the chieftain of a very large tribe which had a monopoly of God's truth.

10   The Bonds of Society

There was nothing which could have ensured the survival of the large society of the age of Charlemagne for long. During the lifetime of Charlemagne it was held together in a loose and uncertain way because of the almost complete absence of powerful enemies. It is true, of course, that no one set of social relations continues without great change for long. Except in a purely biological sense, societies are always short-lived. And since all change in the Middle Ages was much slower than it is in the modern world, Carolingian society existed for quite a few decades. But it could never reach a state of internal equilibrium and therefore gradually ceased to exist, even though it did not succumb to external attack or technological revolution. Within three decades of Charlemagne's death in 814 it had disintegrated because it lost its international character and split up, first into three smaller units, then, within another lifetime, into countless groups, often minutely small.

The forces making for the integration and cohesion of the large society were too weak. The cohesion of clan and kin, the most natural of all forces making for integration, was long absent in most parts of the Empire, except perhaps in Saxony and Bavaria, where tribal traditions lingered on in spite of Christianity. But the inhabitants of a whole empire could never be made to cohere in terms of the principle of a common descent from a heroic or divine ancestor. Clanship had ceased to be a strong bond centuries ago, when the tribes had migrated and when warfare and mobility had forced men to band together as gangs of warriors under a King or chieftain. Another powerful force making for cohesion, the institutionalised feud, was also absent. Many tribes are groups of clans who keep together in a larger unit because they habitually feud with one another. In such cases, the limits of the tribe are defined by the extent of this habit. But here again, the emergence of Charlemagne as the sole ruler had removed this seemingly paradoxical force making for cohesion. Not only had the last descendants of the Merovingian dynasty been successfully eliminated in the preceding generation, but all the various branches of the new dynasty had also been defeated or absorbed. When Charlemagne's brother died two years after his and Charlemagne's succession to power, Charlemagne was left in sole command and the last opportunities for institutionalised political feud disappeared. Rivalry and competition for the highest prize being thus impossible, the inhabitants of the kingdom were no longer kept together by the desire of some local magnates to win it. The consequent absence of civil war, paradoxical though this may seem, weakened rather than strengthened the bonds of society. During Charlemagne's reign there were only two minor

The so-called Talisman of Charlemagne

The King and his courtiers. Utrecht Psalter

rebellions. One was led by a small group of eastern magnates and was easily crushed. The other, more formidable, was focused upon one of Charlemagne's sons; but the conspiracy was discovered before it issued in action. As long as there is bitter competition for the Crown, the Crown is valued. When the competition disappears, this is almost a sure sign that central power is not considered all that desirable.

Fresco fragment from St Sofia, Benevento, Italy, showing a Frankish magnate

Charlemagne, of course, tried very hard to supply a principle of integration and to weld all classes and groups into a single society. We have seen how he tried to streamline the system of royal administration by delegating power and by defining the extent of delegation to counts and bishops; how he instituted a system of supervision by setting up the *missi* and how he tried to strengthen the seat of central authority by erecting his permanent palace in Aix-la-Chapelle. Eventually he even assumed the title of Emperor— though he was most probably aware of how badly his administrative system compared with that of the ancient Roman emperors: he could neither collect taxes from anybody nor dispose of an administrative staff who could read and write. Charlemagne took his duties very seriously and interpreted the patriarchal leadership of David and Moses, whom he sought to imitate, in a very wide manner. He was not devoid of ideas, and the ideological superstructure was provided by St Augustine's *City of God*, a work

Carolingian warriors from the Golden Psalter, St Gall

with which he was well acquainted, and by Alcuin's treatise on kingship entitled *Rhetoric*. From the former he culled the notion that his kingdom and the Church were concentric and identical, and from the latter he derived a notion of virtue, moderation, temperance and the idea that a ruler's behaviour ought to be a model for his subjects.

All this was underpinned by the charismatic institution of divine kingship. The old Merovingian dynasty had been considered the descendants of a mythical hero and had been known as the long-haired Kings because their long hair symbolised a special magic which set them apart from ordinary mortals. When Charlemagne's father removed the last Merovingian King from the throne and took his place, he had sought and obtained the blessing of the Pope and had himself anointed with consecrated oil to make up for the magic of the long hair. He was explicitly King by the Grace of God and the coronation ritual was a very splendid affair, bestowing on the King a divine charisma which no other mortal had. Later generations were to dispute hotly whether by this religious ceremony Charlemagne was placed on the same level as a priest or possibly even above him. But at the time most people did not worry about canonical and legal niceties and the King, as a result of the unction, enjoyed great charismatic power. And Charlemagne's personality was impressive enough to make the most of this charisma. He himself was aware that the power of his personal presence had much to do with the authority by which he held society together. Towards the end of his life he had a dream in which he was presented with a sword on which the following words were inscribed: 'Rat, radoleiba, nasg, ent.' Etymologically they are something of a mystery. But Charlemagne himself interpreted them to mean that now there was plenty, soon there would be deprivation, eventually there would be shortage, and then the end would come. As events were to show, this was by no means a very fanciful interpretation of the history of the kingdom after his death.

The ideological superstructure, the administrative system, and the charismatic power were not sufficient to weld a society together. Social circumstances and economic factors were too much against the formation of an integrated society. The social and economic reality of the age was the large landed estate. It was natural that the owner of every estate should consider himself the sole administrator and beneficiary of his land and the ruler of the people who lived on it. His obligation to his King, his sense of obedience to a central authority, were voluntary. On the estate his authority, delegated to and represented by his stewards, was effective and real. By comparison, the authority of the count or the local bishop was small. Many owners of large estates enjoyed a legally confirmed immunity from the interference of the count who represented royal power. Those who did not, behaved as if they did. For the local count was likely to be their cousin or brother and there was no incentive from him to assert royal authority against his own kinsman.

During the age of Charlemagne the social system known to later historians as 'feudalism' began therefore to make very rapid progress. The poor became tied to the rich, as tenants or serfs, and the rich to the magnates, as vassals. As central authority was distant and ineffectual, and tribal cohesion based on the co-operation of a number of well-defined clans was absent, people tied themselves together as tenants and vassals and lords. Their economic status provided the definition of the rung they were to occupy on the feudal ladder; and an awareness of their own interest and a strong personal sense of loyalty and devotion to the rich man who would protect them provided a strong emotional bond.

The feudal hierarchy, the development of which made such rapid progress during the reign of Charlemagne, was as yet ill-defined. It was not unified and the King was not the apex, the lord of the wealthiest magnates. Instead, a large number of apexes emerged all over the place and, as long as Charlemagne continued to propagate his more ambitious system of centralised administration, the system could indeed not be unified and find in the King its natural apex. For the King preferred to regard his counts and bishops as his officials, not as his tenants-in-chief.

Charlemagne's more splendid attempts at royal government by officials were indeed being overtaken at a fast rate by the spontaneous

Reliquary of Charlemagne's arm, showing Louis the Pious as Emperor

feudalisation of society. Although his own efforts and his ideology were bent upon supplying an alternative, Charlemagne did nothing to actually stem this spontaneous development. The first recorded instance of a feudal ceremony of vassalage is the oath taken by Tassilo of Bavaria to King Pepin, Charlemagne's father, in 757. Tassilo had to make his submission; and Pepin realised that the most effective way of publicising the submission would be by casting it in the mould that was widely known. Tassilo commended himself in vassalage 'by his hands' and swore fealty on the relics of saints 'as becomes a vassal to act towards his lord'. The expression 'by his hands' meant that he knelt and raised his hands as if in prayer and that his lord placed his hands round the vassal's hands. This ritual later became known as 'the mixing of hands'.

Some 30 years later, when Charlemagne was still full of high hopes, he demanded an oath of loyalty from his subjects: he expected no more than that they swear to 'dedicate the days of their lives without fraud or malice to be faithful to their lord King Charles'. Even so, the oath was to be administered only to prominent officials and magnates. All the others were presumably deemed to be committed through their allegiance to the upper classes. But in 802, when Charlemagne was at the height of his power and a wiser and more realistic man, he prescribed another oath; and this time his 'subjects' were told to swear that they would behave to the King as a vassal ought to behave towards his lord. The status of a subject was clearly becoming assimilated to the status of a vassal. It was accepted that the normal state of dependence was that of the vassal; and all those who were not vassals were instructed to behave as if they were.

The assumption of the Imperial title, the exercise of charismatic kingship, the ethical notions of government culled from St Augustine and Cicero were all in vain. The inhabitants of the vast Empire were too illiterate and the means of communication too primitive for Charlemagne's efforts to be effective. The only reality was the landed estate. Whether a man enjoyed his property because he had been invested with it as a royal official, or whether he held it because it was inherited, made no difference. In fact, the office-holders, far from representing royal central authority in each district, used the extra land and extra prestige of their office to steal a march on the other magnates to make themselves into feudal lords. And as they were jockeying for position in every district, more or less clearly defined feudal hierarchies began to emerge. They found their apex not in the men who continued for many generations to call themselves Emperors, but in the most powerful man in each district.

In a very real sense, Charlemagne was the beneficiary of the lull between the age of the migrations of the Teutonic barbarians into the Roman Empire and the age of the feudal monarchies of medieval Europe. In that lull he and his enlightened friends tried to weld people together into a new society. The so-called Carolingian Renaissance which resulted from these efforts, confined as it was to the Court, found no echo in the lives of his subjects, high or low, and bore no relation to the lives they led in their cottages and their estates. It was a grand intention which could not deflect the relentless formation of feudal bonds from their natural path. The copying of manuscripts that took place proved to be beneficial because eventually the ancient originals, written on papyrus gradually disintegrated. These texts would all have been lost to us had they not been copied on parchment by monks. But, in the age in which they were copied, they were not understood. On the other hand, the compositions of homilies, the theological treatises and manuals of instruction were worthy attempts to propagate a system of government and an order of society which could not emerge. They are not only of slight intrinsic interest to us but also of comparative little value to the historian, for they bear so little relation to the actual social conditions of the age.

King David playing the harp before musicians and dancers. The title-page of the Golden Book of Charlemagne

It is not very difficult to see why no social equilibrium could be reached. The two major social tendencies were at cross-purposes with each other. On one side there were the magnates—keen to enlarge their estates and to acquire new ones and to use all opportunities in order to make their neighbours sink into servitude or vassalage. On the other side, there was the King with his ambitious schemes of government and justice culled from Moses and David, St Augustine and Cicero. If these two tendencies had clearly worked *against* each other they might have neutralised each other and led to at least a temporary state of balance. But it so happened that the magnates' appetites did not oppose the King's ambitions and that the King's ambitions countenanced rather than frustrated the magnates' appetites. The magnates supported and urged the King along his path because he led them to conquest and bestowed offices on them—in short created the very opportunities they needed to cross his intention. And the King, in order to be able to govern better, gave the magnates grants of land from the royal domain, supplied them with grants of immunity which legally sanctioned their independence, welcomed the institution of vassalage because it promoted a hierarchical social order and, last but not least, by constant demands for military service created the very conditions which forced the poorer men to seek the 'protection' of the magnates. Materially, the magnates prevailed and it took centuries for new conceptions of government and kingship to emerge in various parts of Charlemagne's Empire. But, ironically, the historical records, laws and chronicles, and the documents of the Carolingian Renaissance which have been left behind, are the records of the drives and institutions which did *not* prevail.

11　Art

The one enduring monument of the age which not only proved influential for centuries to come, but which also has an intrinsic aesthetic interest for us is Carolingian art. The artists of the age did not produce a monumental art. They rarely painted large frescoes or made sculptures. Their technical and material resources were poor. They displayed their craftsmanship and their inventiveness in decorating the many manuscripts that were being copied. Many scribes, when they were copying texts, left blank spaces or whole pages. When their work was done, they handed the book to an illuminator who decorated it by adding ornaments to the initial letters and illustrations on the blank pages. There were very few large buildings which could have been decorated by large paintings and so the whole of the artistic imagination was focused upon manuscripts.

The first thing one can learn from the countless pictures which decorated these manuscripts is that the artists and readers of these manuscripts were preoccupied with only a very small but very distinctive aspect of the Bible. Purely secular subjects, needless to say, were of no interest at all. The one subject which proved of never-ending interest was man's relation to God's plan as it was revealed in the Bible. People thought of the whole of history in terms of three layers. There was the past, as represented by the Old Testament and the history of the ancient Jews. Then there was the present, the Church, founded by Jesus Christ and represented pictorially by the Evangelists or by Jesus Himself. And, finally, there was the future, the promised Second Coming, represented by the Fountain of Life (pp. 129 and 138) or by the Holy Lamb (p. 154).

Many artists tried to give a visual image of the relation between these three layers. The palace at Ingelheim (p. 48) on the Rhine near Mainz was richly decorated and is one of the few examples of a more monumental art. Unfortunately, we know of it only through contemporary descriptions. The palace itself has been in ruins for centuries. The church was decorated on the left wall with scenes from the Old Testament, the

Adoration of the Lamb from the Codex Aureus of St Emmeram

Paradise, the Fall, the Flood, the story of Joseph, Moses on Sinai, the Prophets and the Kings. Opposite, on the right wall, there were the scenes from the New Testament, the Annunciation, the Nativity, the Adoration of the Magi and Christ's Ministry and Passion. The hall of the palace was decorated in a similar pattern, this time with stories taken from secular history. On the left wall there were the ancient kings and heroes; and on the right the 'modern' kings and their achievements, i.e. the foundation of Constantinople, Theodoric the Great, Charles Martel's victories over the pagan Frisians, Pepin's conquest of Aquitaine, Charlemagne's conquest of the Saxons and his coronation in Rome. One might conclude that people tried to understand themselves by studying history comparatively; they believed that the whole course of history had already once run its course in very ancient times and that what had then taken place had prefigured what was taking place now on a higher level. By studying the Old Testament and the history of the ancient kings, one could understand current events. One of the most perfect representations of the three layers of the order of history is to be found in the frontispiece to the Gospels of St Médard of Soissons (p. 155). The bottom of the picture shows a colonnade and behind it, a building. Above it there are four medallions, showing the Evangelists. And at the top there is a picture of the Holy Lamb, adored by the 24 elders. The building at the bottom is

probably a somewhat garbled picture of the cathedral of Aix-la-Chapelle and symbolises the temple of Solomon, that is, the Old Testament; the Evangelists represent the new dispensation and the Holy Lamb symbolises the future, the Second Coming. The internal arrangement of the cathedral in Aix-la-Chapelle was an adaptation of the same idea. On the ground floor there was the altar of Mary, in the gallery the altar of Christ, and on the ceiling an image of God. Efforts were made to use the dimensions of Solomon's temple as indicated in the Bible for the Aix-la-Chapelle cathedral and Charlemagne's throne in

Frontispiece of the Gospels of St Médard of Soissons

the gallery was modelled on that of Solomon.

The frescoes in the church of St John's in Müstair, Grisons, tell a very similar story. In the apses there are pictures of Christ, of St Paul, St Peter, St John and St Stephen. On the back wall there is a picture of the Last Judgment and on the side wall there is a frieze of paintings showing 20 scenes from the life of David and below two friezes, showing 62 events in the life of Jesus. At St Germigny-des-Prés the mosaic in the apse has survived (p. 107). It shows two angels guarding the Ark of the Covenant. Between the angels there is the hand of God, described in the inscription as the 'holy oracle' vouchsafing the Ark which is the symbol of the true faith. The artist went to considerable trouble to present the Ark as faithfully as possible according to the detailed description in Exodus 25:8–22. In the *Libri Carolini* the Ark had been held up as the

one and only artefact directly inspired by God and had been contrasted
to the countless manufactured images, products by human hands, which
were not to be worshipped. The presence of the two angels was a conscious imitation of Solomon's temple as described in the First Book of
Kings and thus the oratory of St Germigny-des-Prés was meant to be
a new temple of Solomon.

There are two things which strike one in the choice of these subjects.
First, the omissions: there is no picture of the Passion on the Cross—
the destroyed painting from Ingelheim is a rare exception and even here
it is improbable that Jesus was represented as suffering. Jesus was seen
as the great hero, the miracle-worker, the victor. The Franks could not
face the fact that he was a down-trodden human being, crucified and
suffering. Indeed, the Frankish King Clovis is reported to have said
that if he and his Franks had been present in Jerusalem at the time, they

Frescoes in St John's, Müstair, Switzerland

157

would not have allowed their lord Jesus to be crucified. This is a very telling comment. It apparently never occurred to the Franks that if they had prevented the Crucifixion they would have deprived the whole of the New Testament of its meaning. Equally important is the absence of personifications and allegories. Neither sun nor moon, neither moral forces nor human emotions were treated allegorically and represented as persons. Art, it was officially laid down in the *Libri Carolini*, had to serve truth. And this meant that art had to portray reality. It had to offer illustrations of what had happened in the past or what had been prophesied. But the artistic imagination was not supposed to run into allegory, let alone surrealism. The second striking thing is that this three-layer vision of the world's history really bears no relation at all to the realities of life and society in the age of Charle-

Ivory bookcover, showing Christ treading the Beasts, and scenes from the Life of Christ

magne. By no stretch of the imagination could anybody who had observed society at the end of the eighth century have argued that it represented the Church under the law dispensed by Christ. In reality it was a very loosely knit society of people who lived according to very primitive lights—banding together at one end of the scale in self-contained manors and villas and, at the other end, under the leadership of a warlord whom they followed into wars against pagans and infidels.

There was, however, one compensating insight. In their cooler moments, Charlemagne and his friends likened themselves to the ancient Jews and saw themselves as a tribe rather than as a church. Hence the great prevalence of illustrations of the Psalter, the frequent pictures of David and Solomon. The artists were, of course, ignorant of what David had really worn. So they depicted him in Frankish dress, as a Frankish King; and, conversely, when they drew a picture of a Frankish King, he seemed indistinguishable from David. In this way there seems to have been present a touch of realism: the Franks under

Celestial map

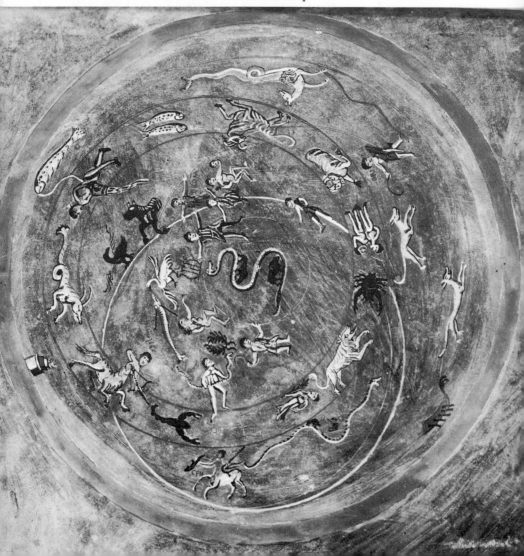

their Kings were more like the Jews under their kings than, for example, the Roman Emperor Constantine surrounded by the bishops who represented a Christian congregation. Therefore, they could cull more from the Old Testament than from the New.

Much less frequent than the representation of history, i.e. of the extension of the world in time, were the representations of the extension of the world in space. The clearest map of the world drawn in the age of Charlemagne was made according to the instructions of the Spanish scholar, Isidore of Seville. The earth was shown as a circle, with the city of Jerusalem at the centre, situated at the bottom of the continent of Asia.

Detail from the Column of Trajan

Below Asia, and separated from it on the left by the River Don and on the right by the River Nile, there were the smaller continents of Europe and Africa, separated from each other by the big ocean which also surrounded the whole circle of continents. Again, the sky appeared on maps, as a circle inside which the signs of the zodiac were marked in a series of eccentric circles (p. 158). According to another map of the sky, the sun and moon were situated in the centre of the circle. They were surrounded by a concentric circle with the signs of the zodiac and by a further concentric circle, containing the figures which represented the planets. It is obvious that none of these maps were intended for

practical purposes but that they were designed to demonstrate the stead-
fast order and harmony of the universe.

The craftsmen of the age of Charlemagne and of the ninth century
combined two artistic traditions. They derived the manner in which
to tell a story, as well as their portraiture, from Late Roman art. We must
go to such examples of Late Roman art as the Column of Trajan in
Rome (p. 159) to see the prototypes of the composition of the pictures
which adorned Carolingian Psalters with representations of the events
of Biblical history. And, in order to find the prototypes of Carolingian
portraits and of the pictures of Christ enthroned in His majesty, we
must go back to Late Roman portraits.

But the Carolingian craftsmen joined another tradition to that of the
Romans and thus created a characteristic style of their own. The
Teutonic and Celtic tribes of pre-Christian Europe had had an art of
their own. But they had never used their craftsmanship in order to
imitate nature or create
representations of natural
objects. Like the art of so
many primitive peoples all
over the earth, their art had
been formal, abstract, geometrical. They delighted in
intricate patterns of lines
and circles which they used
to decorate their ships
(p. 161), their weapons,
their purses (p. 162), their
brooches and clasps. This
geometrical and non-repre-
sentational art had survived
into the Frankish period
and continued to be used
even in the age of Charlemagne for the production of
caskets for relics, for brooches
(pp. 101 and 162) and amulets and for book-covers.

Ivory diptych: the poet and his muse

*Leaf of an ivory diptych:
the consul magnus*

Dragon's head

The men who illustrated Carolingian books brought the Late Roman tradition and the geometrical and abstract tradition together. The figures of Late Roman diptychs (pp. 160 and 161), no matter how clumsy and lifeless they appeared, all showed lingering traces of naturalistic representation of the human form. Even when they were fully or partially clothed, their posture and limbs appear naturalistic. The Carolingian craftsman adopted the habit of representing figures and of placing them against a background and of setting them into a defined surround. But he had no interest in the natural forms of the body. He would not show an unclothed body. But not even the clothing would reveal the natural shape of the body.

The lid of a purse, set with garnets and coloured glass, from Sutton Hoo

Instead, he used the other, geometrical and abstract, tradition in order to explore the countless possibilities of draping the garments over the body. Whatever the surround and the background—the centre-piece of the picture is, first, the face; and second, the cloak. In fact, the cloak is usually more noteworthy than the face. And the cloak is always a most intricate and beautifully designed abstract pattern of folds and pleats. The artists showed a remarkable inventiveness in these patterns and clearly continued the fine tradition of purely geometrical and abstract design of which the splendid ornamental pages from the Lindisfarne Gospel in the British Museum are the most famous example (p. 163). The purely abstract patterns appear also in the Carolingian age in the decorated opening letters of Folchard's Psalter of St Gall (p. 164) or the Second Bible of Charles the Bald of St Denys (p. 164) or in Drogo's Sacramentary of Metz (p. 130) But no

A brooch from Mölsheim

Ornamental page from the Lindisfarne Gospels

matter how satisfying the geometric compositions of these purely abstract works, they are surpassed by the beautiful inventiveness of the designs on the cloaks of Carolingian portraits.

The very earliest examples show the cloak as a purely abstract design which bears no relation to the body it covers. But before long, the designs were adapted and moulded to the body without losing their geometrical patterns. There is a vast array of possibilities for such designs. And we should perhaps survey them, beginning with the picture of St Matthew of the Codex Aureus made in Canterbury about 750. His cloak is an intricate pattern of elongated circular lines. The St Matthew from the Coronation Gospels, of the Aix-la-Chapelle Palace School (before 800), has a cloak which forms a semicircle and which is carefully subdivided by gentle lines flowing towards the centre of the circle (p. 118). The Christ of the Evangelistary of Godescalc, Court School (p. 137), 781–3, shows a cloak which is like a solid trunk. In the middle it is

Initial 'B' from the Second Bible of
Charles the Bald

Initial 'Q' from Folchard's Psalter,
St Gall

dissolved into two sets of circles, each circle centred on one of the knees. The St Matthew of the Gospel Book of Centula, Abbeville, late eighth century, shows a cloak of fairly rigid lines ending in a zigzag pattern below the knees (p. 165). Its stiffness and angularity gives the impression that it is broken off, rather than drawn. The St John of the Lorsch Gospel Book, Palace School, 810 has a cloak with straight lines running from the left hip to the right arm and right leg. But the sub-division by lines is overlaid by a playful pattern of round circles printed on the cloth.

It seems that there was a parting of ways. In the Palace School, artists tended to loosen their lines (p. 111) and in another school, patronised by Ada, supposed to have been a sister of Charlemagne, they made them more and more rigid, even though the garment had flowing folds. The artist who created the pictures in the Gospel Book of Archbishop Ebo of Reims (before 823) followed the Palace School and introduced a further original variation. His St Matthew's cloak (p. 166) is a semicircle broken up by countless quivering lines. It is as if his hand had trembled when he was drawing the folds and thus he managed to give the Evangelist an expression of feverish inspiration as he is writing his Gospel. And, like a true artist, he carried the quivering lines beyond the outlines of the central cloak: St Matthew's hair and toes, the hill-side and the trees in the background, all show the same quivering and electrified vivacity. The same style of quivering

St Matthew from the Centula Gospel

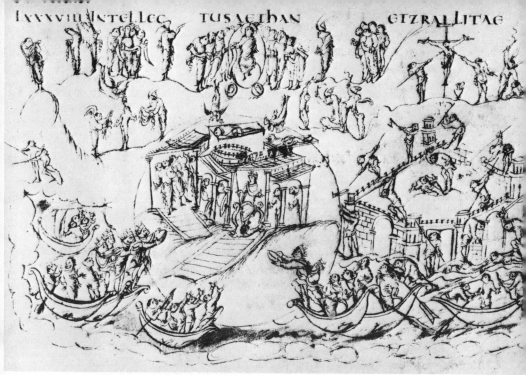

Various scenes from the Utrecht Psalter, illustrating Psalm 88

excitement was used by the artist who drew the pictures for the Utrecht Psalter in about 820 (p. 167). His scenes show a frantic activity, the people have a wild gaze and the bodies lean either forward or backward. It is as if this artist had carried the idea of quivering lines beyond the stage of formal design of one static figure and had used it for the composition as a whole.

The confluence of the two traditions, the Roman motif and the Teutonic and Celtic love of the geometrical design, produced great art. It fails to inspire us in the way in which the personal devotion of a Fra Angelico or the personal agonies portrayed by Michelangelo or El Greco inspire us. It is an art which is used for didactic purposes rather than as a vehicle of individual and personal feeling. But like all genuine art it shows that beauty is a function of form and not of the naturalness of representation. The Carolingian artists, standing at the very point where Roman and Teutonic and Celtic traditions of craftsmanship came together, were in a unique position to create artistic beauty.

And yet a word of caution ought to be added. Almost invariably,

St Matthew from the Gospel Book of Archbishop Ebo of Reims

reproduction of works of art detracts from the power and beauty of the original. With Carolingian art, the opposite is true. The printed reproduction always gives a neater and more perfect impression than the original. The original is obviously drawn by hand and tinted with colours which do not flow evenly on the parchment or vellum. The chemical composition of the inks and tints posed a technical problem which the craftsmen of the period could not master. The originals, therefore, all exhibit a primitive technique—which is a great source of charm but which is oddly out of step with the perfection of formal composition.

This technical deficiency is only a minor example of the enormous technical deficiency of the system of Carolingian society as a whole. At every step we have observed how the intentions of the governors, informed by Roman and Christian ideals, were curiously out of step with the social and economic realities of the age. But if one makes an allowance for the technical deficiency of the art, one must grant that in art something was made possible which was denied to the aspirations of Charlemagne's government. In art, and in art alone, a genuine fusion of the traditions of the ancient world and the world of the Teutonic and Celtic tribesmen was brought about. And this fusion, unlike the administrative schemes of Charlemagne's 'Imperial' government, not only survived the age but laid the foundations for the art of the succeeding centuries. It seems, therefore, proper to end this picture of society in the age of Charlemagne with a quotation from Santayana: 'After life is over and the world has gone up in smoke, what realities might the spirit in us still call its own without illusion save the form of those very illusions which have made up our story.'

Suggestions for further reading

J. Beckwith, *Early Medieval Art*, London, 1964.

M. Bloch, *French Rural History* (translation by J. Sondheimer), London, 1966.

D. Bullough, *The Age of Charlemagne*, London, 1965.

E. S. Duckett, *Alcuin, Friend of Charlemagne*, New York, 1951.

Einhard, *The Life of Charlemagne* (translation by S. E. Turner), Ann Arbor, 1960.

H. Fichtenau, *The Carolingian Empire* (translation by P. Munz), Oxford, 1957.

F. L. Ganshof, 'Charlemagne', *Speculum*, XXIV, 1949.

F. L. Ganshof, 'The Impact of Charlemagne on the Institutions of the Frankish Realm', *Speculum*, XL, 1965.

R. Hinks, *Carolingian Art*, London, 1935.

M. L. W. Laistner, *Thought and Letters in Western Europe, A.D. 500–900*, new ed., London, 1957.

R. Latouche, *The Birth of Western Economy* (translation by E. M. Wilkinson), London, 1961.

P. Munz, *The Origin of the Carolingian Empire*, Dunedin and Leicester, 1960.

P. Munz, *The End of the Ancient World*, Historical Studies, XI, 1963.

H. Pirenne, *Mohammed and Charlemagne* (translation by B. Miall), London, 1939.

W. Ullmann, *The Growth of Papal Government in the Middle Ages*, London, 1955.

J. M. Wallace-Hadrill, *The Barbarian West*, London, 1952.

L. Wallach, *Alcuin and Charlemagne*, Ithaca, 1959.

Index

The numerals in **bold type** refer to the page on which illustrations appear.